Arguments

WITH THE World

Barb,
Merry Christmas
1992.
much love
Lish.

OTHER ESSAYS FROM QUARRY PRESS

Arguments WITH THE World

ESSAYS BY
BRONWEN WALLACE

Edited By
JOANNE PAGE

QUARRY PRESS

The publisher acknowledges the financial assistance of The Canada Council and the Ontario Arts Council.

Canadian Cataloguing in Publication Data

Wallace, Bronwen
    Arguments with the World
    ISBN 1–55082–040–0

    I. Page, Joanne II. Title.
PS8595.A56504A84 1992 C814'.54 C92–090058–5
PR9199.3.W35A74 1992

Cover art by Mary Pratt entitled "In My Mother's House," reproduced by permission of the artist.
Design by Keith Abraham. Typeset by Susan Hannah.
Printed and bound in Canada by Hignell Printing, Winnipeg, Manitoba.
Published by *Quarry Press Inc.*, P.O. Box 1061, Kingston, Ontario K7L 4Y5.

Contents

Foreword

As a poet who writes rhetorical essays, I appreciate the public voice that the craft requires, a way of articulating a clear position on events and issues. As a political person who writes poetry, I know the need for the intimate, inner argument that is the center of the poem — Bronwen Wallace.

"A wonderful poet is gone," Dennis Lee wrote when Bronwen Wallace died of cancer in 1989. Lee was correct, but it wasn't that simple. We've been cheated of the poems and stories Bronwen would have written, yes, but we also lost a passionate non-fiction writer who sought to change the world. Until now her non-fiction prose has been unknown to readers outside Kingston, Ontario, certainly unavailable as a body of work.

Writing, politics, her own life: all are synthesized in her non-fiction. Much of the material in this collection originated in essays that appeared as the column "In Other Words," in the Kingston *Whig-Standard*, which she launched in May 1987 in response to a request from the Kingston women's community that she bring their voice to the pages of the newspaper. Except for a three month break in the fall of 1988 when she was writer-in-residence at the University of

Western Ontario, the column ran uninterrupted until the end of February 1989. Bronwen's voice resonates like a struck bell through the issues of her day, issues still ours.

Once Bronwen and I were walking in downtown Kingston on our way to the library, sharing information about and opinions on a local strike. As we negotiated an ice patch on Earl Street, she interrupted our conversation to explain how she had to be careful because of her knee, which led to a discussion of arthritis and how it runs in families, then a few words about feet and what a hard time we had finding comfortable shoes. A bunch of high-school kids streamed around us; they all had a word with her. Setting off again, we were sizzling through a discussion of 'voice appropriation' in stories when we met a guy she knew; he simply had to tell her about a book he'd read on animal neurology — and about a movie she should see. We progressed half a block more and two women called across the street to remind her of a demonstration on the weekend. And so it went, all the way to the library. And so it seemed always to go with Bronwen, with her thinking, with her writing.

Bronwen's prose changes direction in the apparently effortless way a woman will comfort a child, stir the soup, pick up laundry, write a shopping list, and remind herself to phone her mother. She writes eagerly, infectiously. The pleasure of sharing discoveries spills into the sentences: look at *this* and *this*. It's a measure of her skill and of the respect she had for her readers that we never feel the heavy hand of writerly authority. Instead we hear the comfortable voice of an old friend, one who regularly drops by for coffee and doesn't mind the clattering of dishes in the background. Attention to detail threaded her life together and makes her writing precisely observed. She has the poet's gift of tucking the unexpected, perfect metaphor into a sentence, leaving the reader with caught breath.

Born in 1945, Bronwen's political awakening came early with, among other things, a high-school newspaper called *Thot*. When the local school board took exception to its content, the irony of educators banning thought did not escape her. She went on to become a campus radical. In 1970 she made an impassioned pro-choice speech from among a group of protestors chained to the visitors' gallery of the House of Commons. The same year she abandoned graduate work in English at Queen's University in Kingston and made her way across Canada, eventually settling in Windsor with her partner Ron Baxter. There she was active in a women's co-op bookstore, protests, union organizing and, when their son Jeremy arrived, in co-op daycare. She wrote about issues one friend describes as "grounded in the men and women who worked in the factories, people who worked with their hands."

Attaching people, weaving them together was Bronwen's great delight. Much was sheer Bronwen: generosity, scarves and earrings, cures, outrage, curiosity, gardens. And just as distinctive was her sense of place, or "location," to use her term. By location she meant home, the center, a roof over the heart. She loved the implications of home, how it was more than shelter, how it mixed family history, daily life, friends, chili sauce recipes, the patches of earth that are peculiar to each of us. Bronwen located herself in the hardscrabble farms and lakes of southeastern Ontario, identifying herself with her grandmother's runaway horse, tears on a friend's cheeks, her father's Sunday grace, lemon balm and green tomatoes, Jeremy's bike, an Emmylou Harris song, her mother's stories. She anchored herself in this commotion of past and present. Her territory, in writing as in life, was like the eastern Ontario landscape she loved so well — the immutable realities that lie like bedrock beneath the ordinary dailiness of life.

Family, politics, work, landscape: she had all the ingredients. With encouragement from the poet Phil Hall, Bronwen began to find her distinctive literary voice. By the time her first volume of poetry came out in 1980 (*Marrying into the Family*), Bronwen and Jeremy were back in Kingston. In the next nine years she hit her stride. Three books — *Signs of the Former Tenant*, *Common Magic*, and *The Stubborn Particulars of Grace* — followed in close succession.

She and her partner Chris Whynot made two documentary films: *All You Have To Do* in 1982, a sensitive depiction of a close friend's battle with Hodgkin's Disease, and *That's Why I'm Talking* in 1984, a look at four contemporary Canadian poets — Pier Giorgio di Cicco, Mary di Michele, Robert Priest, and Carolyn Smart. She helped establish the Women's Studies Program at Queen's University and brought a new perspective to the English Department's Creative Writing program. She gave writing workshops in schools, at summer writing courses, and in her own home.

In the mid-1980s Bronwen worked as a front-line counselor at Kingston Interval House, a shelter for battered women and their children. The two year stint moved her profoundly, temporarily dried up her writing, and crystalized her feminist politics, which found voice in 1987 when she began writing "In Other Words," for the Kingston *Whig-Standard*. At the same time, she completed two manuscripts which were published posthumously: *People You'd Trust Your Life To*, a volume of short stories, and *Keep That Candle Burning Bright and Other Poems*. Bronwen grew to be regarded as a combined hell-raiser and conscience of the various communities in which she moved. This kind of public presence can paralyze a writer. At the very least it's a burden. Bronwen carried it lightly — which looks easy but requires discipline — leavening the mix with a healthy shot of irreverence. However seriously others took her, she regarded herself as just another women doing the best she could, just another woman "keeping on."

Bronwen was a mother, lover, friend, daughter, sister, and mentor. She was also a feminist and a long-time political activist. She required no more than a person could give. She assumed you would do your best, one of those absolutely simple attitudes which is at the same time enabling and merciful. Feisty and compassionate, tolerant and challenging, she wrote the way she spoke. What she had to say was always principled, often unexpected. Her finger on a particular situation, she'd explain its complicated social context, and then go on to wonder what would happen if the situation were reversed, if the assumptions were different. She didn't provide answers. In questioning, she knew, lay the pathway to change.

At the same time, she didn't turn away from uncomfortable truths. She fashioned her own dying into a rich communal ceremony that sought to comfort her friends and family. To the end she remained deeply engaged with the grief of those she loved, and with the pain and mystery of leaving them.

Bronwen's prose is home to surprise, anger, teasing, sleeve-tugging, and always to questions like "who wins here?" or "do you believe that?" She writes out of a tough reasonableness that allows imperfections but demands fairness. Bronwen discusses the politics of power and exclusion, goddesses and reproductive rights, women lost and found, nurturing children, and the crafting of poems, and much more. All bear her hallmark: incisive writing and a wonderfully wicked laugh.

This book is divided into three parts, with an Introduction and a Coda. A set of "Morningside" chats with Peter Gzowski provides a general introduction to the political and literary overlap of Bronwen's life. "The Politics of Everyday" is a pithy and accessible look at everything from gender issues to Free Trade. "The Family and Other Stories" examines, among other things, how we define our families and how these definitions affect individuals and society at large. "Arguments with Myself" is a meditation on and celebration of the writing life, featuring an interview with critic Janice Williamson. The Coda, "Blueprints for a Larger Life," serves as a final look at Bronwen's philosophy. A keynote address delivered to a large audience on International Women's Day just days after she had been diagnosed with cancer, "Blueprints" was Bronwen's final public appearance, although nobody knew it at the time. It remains an unforgettable event for those who were there, testimony to her fierce mind and shining, caring heart.

Joanne Page

Introduction:
The Morningside Interviews

1

PETER GZOWSKI: Every Monday morning at this time, we go to a Canadian poet to find out what he — or in this case, *she* — is writing about, thinking about. This morning, the Kingston, Ontario poet, Bronwen Wallace. She's on the line from her home. Good morning, Bronwen.

BRONWEN WALLACE: Good morning, Peter. And how are you this morning?

PG: Not that bad.

BW: Well, I'm feeling really good this morning because school's started again, and for me September is always a mixed emotions kind of month. Because on the one hand the house is quiet and I'm free to start writing again after the summer holidays, and on the other hand I can remember how I felt as a child, going off to school and not really wanting to be there, and I'm feeling sorry for my son, who's in that position. So the poem I want to read this morning is a poem about how [*Pause*] whenever a woman, I think, starts trying to do her own kind of work, this work gets tangled up in domestic life around her. And it's a poem that's dedicated to Virginia Woolf, because Virginia Woolf said that all we needed was a room of our own — although I've come to think it's a little more complicated

■ II ■

than that. The poem's called "A Simple Poem for Virginia Woolf."
PG: Do you want to do it?
BW: I sure do.

> This started out as a simple poem
> for Virginia Woolf   you know the kind
> we women writers write these days
> in our own rooms
> on our own time
> a salute   a gesture of friendship
> a psychological debt
> paid off
> I wanted it simple
> and perfectly round
> hard as an
> egg   I thought
> only once I'd said egg
> I thought of the smell
> of bacon grease and dirty frying-pans
> and whether there were enough for breakfast
> I couldn't help it
> I wanted the poem to be carefree and easy
> like children playing in the snow
> I didn't mean to mention
> the price of snowsuits or
> how even on the most expensive ones
> the zippers always snag
> just when you're late for work
> and trying to get the children
> off to school on time
> a straightforward poem
> for Virginia Woolf   that's all
> I wanted really
> not something tangled in
> domestic life the way

Jane Austen's novels tangled
with her knitting her embroidery
whatever it was she hid them under
I didn't mean to go into all that
didn't intend to get confessional
and tell you how
every time I read a good poem
by a woman writer I'm always peeking
behind it trying to see
if she's still married
or has a lover at least
wanting to know what she did
with her kids while she wrote it
or whether she had any
and if she didn't if she'd chosen
not to or if she did did she
choose and why   I didn't mean
to bother with that
and I certainly wasn't going
to tell you about the time
my best friend was sick in intensive care
and I went down to see her
but they wouldn't let me in
because I wasn't her husband
or her father   her mother
I wasn't family
I was just her friend
and the friendship of women
wasn't mentioned
in hospital policy
or how I went out and kicked
a dent in the fender of my car
and sat there crying because
if she died I wouldn't be able
to tell her how much I loved her

(though she didn't and we laugh
about it now) but that's what got me
started I suppose   wanting to write
a gesture of friendship
for a woman for a woman writer
for Virginia Woolf
and thinking I could do it
easily   separating the words
from the lives they come from
that's what a good poem should do
after all and I wasn't going to make excuses
for being a woman   blaming years of silence
for leaving us
so much to say

This started out as a simple poem
for Virginia Woolf
it wasn't going to mention history
or choices or women's lives
the complexities of women's friendships
or the countless gritty details
of an ordinary woman's life
that never appear in poems at all
yet even as I write these words
those ordinary details intervene
between the poem I meant to write
and this one   where the delicate faces
of my children   faces of friends
of women I have never even seen
glow on the blank pages
and deeper than any silence
press around me
waiting their turn

PG: That's Bronwen Wallace, with a poem called "A Simple Poem for Virginia Woolf." It's from Bronwen Wallace's new collection of poems, and the collection is called *Signs of the Former Tenant*. It's published by Oberon; Bronwen Wallace speaking to us from her home in Kingston. How does a poet now spend her morning, having launched the *Morningside* week?

BW: I think I'll start with a second or third cup of coffee . . . (*Laughs*).

PG: Just like most of the rest of the world.

BW: That's right. It takes a while to get the brain ticking, you know. My son has been very quiet for the last ten minutes, so we'll have a few minutes together before he starts off for school.

PG: At least one of the children you talk of *is* going to school.

BW: Yes he is; he'll be there. No truant officers needed here.

12 September 1983

2

PETER GZOWSKI: The poetry of Bronwen Wallace honors a part of this country that's had its share of happiness and heartaches — the Ottawa Valley around Kingston, Ontario has provided an uneasy home to centuries of Scottish and Irish settlers who have clung to the land which itself clings to rocks. Bronwen Wallace has a new book of poetry; it's called *Common Magic*, and she joins me in the studio this morning. Good morning.

BRONWEN WALLACE: Good morning.

PG: I know what it's like there, you know. My family had — do you know where Hillier is?

BW: Yeah.

PG: Hillier isn't as rocky as your part of it, 'cause you go farther north. It's the rocks that you . . .

BW: It's the rocks because I see the rocks as the major configuration of the landscape, and the farms are just sort of these lucky little deposits that made it, somehow.

PG: Did the people who settled it know that under all those trees there were rocks?

BW: Actually, I was researching this, and somebody in the Queen's Geography Department told me that when the first settlers came over here, they were under the impression — because of their experience in Scotland — that a heavily wooded area was very fertile. So, not knowing that trees could grow on rocks in Canada, they picked the really heavily wooded stuff, and when they got the land cleared, they found that they had picked a mountain, basically. But being Scots Presbyterians they stayed.

PG: And planted lilacs: now, see, I can't remember which poem this is from, but there's one poem in which you point out that the lilacs that are there are the external sign of happiness . . .

BW: Yeah, and good luck. Actually they brought them over with them, very often, and planted them as a sign of good luck beside the door-post.

PG: So you might think that it's a spontaneous gesture of nature, but it's the settlers themselves. I don't know why I'm beginning by talking about the geographical location because the poems in the book are about so much more. And yet, it's all right there. When you grew up there, were you aware of the kind of country you were growing up in?

BW: I think I must have been. Although when I think about it now, I think there's a line in a story by Alice Munro about driving with her mother — and this is a different part of Ontario — but she says we drove through country that we didn't know we loved. And I think that's what it's been for me as I grew older: realizing that I really *did* love this landscape and I really *had* looked at it, but I didn't realize that when I was growing up. And to some extent, that's what those poems are about: suddenly realizing that I've been looking at this landscape all along, but not really seeing it. Or not really seeing what I am in relation to it.

PG: And the people in relation to it. [*Reads:*] ". . . farmlands draw their nourishment / from an ancient mountain range, / and houses rise, insistent / as the rock and almost as indifferent." That's you.

These are stubborn people as well as a stubborn land.

BW: Yeah, I think so.

PG: Are you of that stock?

BW: I certainly am, in terms of my heritage. My father's family has lived on the same farm for about a hundred and fifty, almost two hundred years. And my mother's people were all United Empire Loyalists . . .

PG: U.E.L.s, eh?

BW: U.E.L.s, yeah (*Laughs*).

PG: Did your grandfather never really venture more than twenty miles from . . .

BW: No, that is actually a grandfather of a friend of mine, who never went to Montreal or Toronto. I think my grandfather did travel a little bit, but there were certainly lots of other elderly people who didn't. I think my grandfather did, but this other person's grandfather — who became *any* grandfather in the poem — never did.

PG: Why do you live there? Because you have lived elsewhere, and have chosen to go back.

BW: Ah . . . I like it. I can give you all the other reasons: it's cheap, it's easy to get jobs because I know lots of people, it's relatively clean, it's beautiful in the summertime. But I think it comes down to the fact that this is where I like to live. I love it.

PG: You didn't say the light, you didn't say the lake. But you did say the cost of housing . . .

BW: (*Laughs*) This is the eighties, I have to get down to the *real* thing . . .

PG: But that's so, if I dare say this, that's such a Canadian thing you just said. I mean we all live where we live. And this is your turf.

BW: And in a sense this is what I have to come to terms with. I suppose I'm doing the same thing that my great-great-great-great grandmother did: well, this is where I *am*, this is what I come to terms with. And not seeing that as a limitation that inhibits me, but as a limitation that enlarges me in some way.

PG: Is that the kind of thing you figure out after you've done something, or am I hearing something that you would have actually thought through rationally, and said 'I'm going back to Kingston because it's a limitation that frees me?' You wouldn't have said that, would you? Or because 'I know a house I can rent for six hundred dollars? or three hundred?'

BW: . . . And so-and-so who knows that I'm James Wallace's grand-daughter will give me a job, so . . . I'll go back.

PG: What's the job, because you work from nine to five, sometimes?

BW: Sometimes . . . I've worked as a teacher, I've worked as a secretary. In my most recent job, I worked as a counselor at a crisis center for battered women — Kingston Interval House, actually — for almost two years. I just stopped that job in October, and I'm on tax-payer's money right now, on UIC and a little bit of Canada Council money.

PG: I want to talk to you about that, about the way you write poetry while you're doing that, but even as you say it, there's a poem that we're about to ask you to read which is about those women, and their men, and it obviously grows. [*Pause*] I mean, it's something that you've learned. Do you want to read the poem? Because there's so much *in* there . . .

BW: Sure. Sure. Because it really is about what I learned from them, very specifically. It's called "Thinking with the Heart," and it begins with two quotations, one of which is from the American photographer Diane Arbus. "I worked from awkwardness. By that I mean I don't like to arrange things. If I stand in front of something, instead of arranging it, I arrange myself." And the other comment comes from a Kingston cop: "The problem with you women is, you think with your hearts."

> How else to say it
> except that the body is a limit
> I must learn to love,
> that thought is no different from flesh
> or the blue pulse that rivers my hands.
> How else, except to permit myself

this heart and its seasons,
like the cycles of the moon
which never seem to get me anywhere
but back again, not out.

Thought should be linear.
That's what the policeman means
when I bring the woman to him,
what he has to offer for her bruises, the cut
over her eye: *charge him or we can't help you.*
He's seen it all before anyway. He knows
how the law changes, depending on what you think.
It used to be a man could beat his wife
if he had to; now, sometimes he can't
but she has to charge him
and nine times out of ten
these women who come in here
ready to get the bastard
will be back in a week or so
wanting to drop the whole thing
because they're back together,
which just means a lot of paperwork
and running around for nothing.
It drives him crazy, how a woman
can't make up her mind and stick to it,
get the guy out once and for all.
'Charge him,' he says 'or we won't help.'

Out of her bed then, her house, her life,
but not her head, no, nor her children,
out from under her skin.
Not out of her heart, which goes on
in its slow, dark way, wanting
whatever it is hearts want

when they think like this;
a change in his, probably,
a way to hold what the heart can't
without breaking: how the man who beats her
is also the man she loves.

I wish I could show you
what a man's anger makes
of a woman's face,
or measure the days it takes
for her to emerge from a map of bruises
the colour of death. I wish there were words
that went deeper than *pain* or *terror*
for the place that woman's eyes can take you
when all you can hear
is the sound the heart makes
with what it knows of itself
and its web of blood.

But right now, the policeman's waiting
for the woman to decide.
That's how he thinks of it; *choice*
or how you can always get what you want
if you want it badly enough.
Everything else he ignores,
like the grip of his own heart's red
persistent warning that he too is fragile.
He thinks he thinks with his brain
as if it were safe up there
in its helmet of bone
away from all that messy business
of his stomach or his lungs.
And when he thinks like that
he loses himself forever.

But perhaps you think I'm being hard on him,
he's only doing his job after all,
only trying to help.
Or perhaps I'm making too much of the heart,
pear-shaped and muscular, a pump really,
when what you want is an explanation or a reason.
But how else can I say it?
Whatever it is you need
is what you must let go of now
to enter your body
just as you'd enter the room where the woman sat
after it was all over,
hugging her knees to her chest,
holding herself as she'd hold her husband
or their children, *for dear life*,
feeling the arm's limit, bone and muscle,
like the heart's.
Whatever you hear then
crying through your own four rooms,
what you must name for yourself
before you can love anything at all.

PG: I don't think you're being too hard on him. That's . . . in fact,
you know I've never seen that. I've never seen those bruises or those
eyes that you describe so . . . powerfully. And I don't understand it.
And I sense that *you* don't understand . . . yet.

BW: No. I think that what we're facing as a society, in a way, is that
we don't understand it, and it would be really nice to think that it's
happening over there to just a few people — you know — that it's
not something that we've all created out of the way we've chosen to
live. Which is partly, I think, maybe what I was coming — beginning
to come to — in that poem: this isn't an anomaly, this isn't something we can have a fixed decision on, you know, this affects us all,
we all have to come to terms with it.

PG: What took you to that job?

BW: I had come to the point, actually, of feeling that I really wanted to get involved in something down to earth and nitty-gritty. I was trying to decide what that would be, what kind of job I would take next. And I received a call from a close friend of mine, somebody whom I had always perceived as being *extremely* together, who in fact had been battered, and had been battered so badly that she had almost been killed. And that seemed to me to be a message about what I should do. And so I started volunteering at Kingston Interval House and before long I was working there.

PG: What did you think of it before . . .

BW: What did I think of before I ever started working there? I think I thought what most people thought, which was that the people who got involved in that were sick people, that is wasn't very widespread, that it just happened to, you know, maybe to women on welfare or to people who drank, or something like that. And that it was cut and dried: that anybody who stayed in that situation was an idiot.

PG: All you have to do is leave.

BW: Even if it's twenty below zero and you've got four kids and no money: simple.

PG: How did you find out that it isn't simple? How did your views change?

BW: By listening. By listening very carefully to the women at the House, and by realizing that a lot of what I had always interpreted as 'excuses,' in terms of the arguments they would make for going back, or choices they had made about why they stayed — were in fact survival strategies. That they weren't totally victims and they weren't totally passive. That they *were* trying to work their way through this situation, but that they had to do it *their* way. And that it *wasn't* a black and white issue. And just hearing stories over and over again and seeing people make different choices and seeing them *wanting* to make one choice and being *forced* to make another because something as simple as the mother's allowance check didn't come on time. Or one of the kids got sick so they had to go back. Or they didn't get the apartment they had hoped. And just seeing that there are so many factors in even the SMALLEST choice that it isn't easy.

PG: Did you meet the men, there?

BW: Not very often. Sometimes they'd come to the door, sometimes they'd phone. But one of the things about the House was that the women who came there were guaranteed that it was safe.

PG: How would you deal with . . .

BW: With the men? I'd deal with them, actually, the way a friend of mine in Kingston has just started dealing with them. A man who himself, I think, at one point was fairly violent, who has now begun a group for batterers. And I think one starts with the premise that people can change. And that if a woman has a choice to leave, a man has a choice to find another way besides violence to deal with conflict. And once a person realizes that they can change, then it's talking about how to change your behavior, basically. Because I think that men who batter also have a lot of problems themselves, in terms of choosing violence as a way of controlling people, feeling that they have to be in control all the time. They tend to have pretty stereotyped ideas about men's and women's roles. And a lot of the work that's done with batterers is just getting them to see that they *can't* be in control all the time, and that being in control doesn't mean that you're safe, necessarily. I think the main message is that we're not totally the victims of our society or the victims of our past or the victims of our biology or anything else. That we can choose, that we can make changes.

PG: What's different between the Bronwen Wallace who just told me that in answer to a direct question, and who said it with emotion and really thought it through, and the Bronwen Wallace who wrote a poem based on the same experience? What's the difference? What is a poet *doing*?

BW: When I was working on this book I had a little quotation from Yeats up above my desk. I know I'll misquote it, but it's something like 'the argument I have with others I call rhetoric. The argument I have with myself is poetry.' And it seems to me that if I am going to be on a panel on domestic violence, I can make *these* sort of statements, but when I come to think about violence as a poet, then I have to go into it in a much different way. Because I have to have discussion or argument or a debate with myself about it. In part, "Thinking with the Heart" is about that. It's really a mulling-it-over at another level, and then finding a way to put that on the page in a way through the images and the language that I use that will at least begin that process in you, when you read it.

PG: Do you recollect in tranquillity?

BW: Oh. *Yeah.* [*Pause*]

PG: There's so much heavy stuff in the book. But you're not a heavy person. And damn if I can resist saying that they're not heavy poems. I don't know how I can say that, but there is something about your poetry that takes the curse off these things.

BW: I hope so. Because that's what I was trying to do. I really do believe that in recognizing them, in really looking at them, they become part of our experience and then we can decide what we're going to do about them.

PG: Where's the hope? Change?

BW: Yeah. The fact that we have a cerebral cortex and a heart (*Laughs*). And we can use them both. And we're not victims. We can still choose. We're still here.

PG: There's a lot left to talk to you about. I wish you wouldn't just only come down here when you bring new books. You did one poem for us, years ago, and I really like that too.

BW: That was in *Signs* — the Virginia Woolf poem. That's right.

PG: This is a wonderful book of poems. It's called *Common Magic*, and Bronwen Wallace is the poet. The book is published by Oberon. We'll get you back here; I'm not waiting till you do another book. Okay?

BW: Okay, thank you.

14 March 1986

▪ I ▪

The Politics of Everyday

■ ■ ■ ■ ■

The Cuban Missile Crisis and Me

I must admit I was more than a little nervous when I was asked to be the after-dinner speaker tonight. I was told my talk should be "witty, entertaining and enlightening," and that I had to do it in front of a bunch of history teachers. Now, I should warn you that my knowledge of history seldom rises far enough above the layperson's usual miss-mash of half-facts to earn me the yellow wedge in a Trivial Pursuit game. I mean, I know a couple of treaties, and I remember who said things like "The Buck Stops Here"(though not who said "Conscription if necessary, though not necessarily conscription") but that's about it. So much for enlightenment.

On the other two requirements, wit and entertainment, I also feel inadequate. I spend most of my time writing poetry, or, more likely these days, a collection of short stories. I spend a lot of time alone, staring out the window, moodily drinking coffee. Being asked to give a speech, of all things, is essentially being asked to do the very thing that I work hard all my life trying to avoid. And that is having to speak, out loud, on my feet, in person to a crowd of strangers. I prefer to do my speaking to strangers in print, preferably after several months of revisions.

But this, of course, is why writers like myself get asked to be speakers at functions like this one. We appear so articulate on the page that people think we're like that in real life. And so we get to be experts in all sorts of things we actually know absolutely nothing about simply because we have the gift of gab.

However, I did accept this invitation, I've had a free meal and I'm getting an honorarium out of the History Department, so I suppose I have to say something, preferably historical, maybe even feminist, that will enlighten and entertain you for a few minutes more.

Perhaps a good place to start would be to ask myself what I'm doing here, as a poet, a feminist poet, in fact, talking to a bunch of secondary school history teachers. Besides the fact that I was asked, I mean, besides the free meal and the honorarium, why did I accept?

When I think about it that way I realize that my being here is the result of a coincidence between a historical event of great political significance in the public world and one of equally great, albeit private and personal significance in my own. And it strikes me that it might be a useful exercise for me to trace the history of my journey from that coincidence to this evening as a way of illustrating some ideas about the nature of history and the teaching of it which are of vital importance to me and will, I hope, be of relevance to you.

How did I get to be a feminist poet talking to a bunch of history teachers? First of all, I am not so naive or simplistic as to think that only one event got me here. I'm a poet because I had a mother who read to me, a score of supportive English teachers, both male and female, and I guess a natural talent. But I am a particular kind of poet and one whose themes follow a particular bent because of a revelation. An epiphany, if you will, that I can pinpoint with absolute accuracy. The date was October 24, 1962. The place was my grade thirteen history class, taught by Mr. Harold Ritchie at Kingston Collegiate & Vocational Institute. The event was the Cuban Missile Crisis.

Now, I don't think I can get away with saying that I am here as a feminist poet talking to a bunch of history teachers because of the Cuban Missile Crisis without explaining a little more. So I will, because it is my belief that it is in the explanation, in the interpretation of events, *in the way that we use them in our personal lives* that history begins to matter.

So here we go. I must admit that though I liked Mr. Ritchie and I enjoyed his class, history was not a big deal for me. Mostly I memorized. I was good at this and it was easy to get high marks without having to think, a talent, I've noticed, that a great many powerful people employ in situations far more significant to most of us than high school history classes. Another reason why I wasn't too interested in history class was that it didn't ever really come home to me that what I learned there had anything, ever, at all, to do with me personally. It was dates and wars and men signing treaties and finding countries and blah, blah, blah.

What mattered to me in my grade 13 history class in 1962 was that I sat beside a guy named R. T. These are his initials, since I don't think it's fair to him (or to me) to give you his full name. R. T. was new at our school that year. Every girl I knew had a thing for him, and I, though I had a perfectly nice, good-looking steady boyfriend of my own, was madly in love with him. What I remember most is that he always wore his shirts rolled up about three rolls on his arms and I could become quite mesmerized by the way the sunlight from the window shone on the fine hairs on his arm. I also remember — with absolute clarity — that he smelled of starch and Lifebuoy soap, a combination that returns him to me still, whenever I smell it. If I had known the word *erotic*, which I didn't in 1962, I would have relished my feelings for R. T. as the first real experience of that sort. Even without knowing the word, I relished it, though what we did all period was pass notes about our respective girl- and boyfriend, old Mr. Ritchie, the football game or whatever. We were good friends. That was it.

All of which implies, truthfully, that I never much listened in History class, what with the smell of R. T. and being 17 and the endless drone of dates and treaties, it didn't seem to matter, though I know that Mr. Ritchie was a good teacher, even before the revelation. I mean, I can actually remember other things he said on other days, though not as clearly.

So on October 24 R. T. and I are sitting there, and I'm watching the light on his wrist hairs, and smelling his smell, and dreaming away, when Mr. Ritchie comes in, and the class gets quiet, and I figure it'll be more of the same, whatever we were studying that year, which to tell you the truth I forget.

But that's not what happened.

Instead, Mr. Ritchie came in very quietly, closed the door, and said, again very quietly, "This may be the last history class we will ever have together."

He may have even said something about it being the last history class anyone would ever have, but I could be making that part up.

What happened next was that he began to talk to us about the blockade and Kennedy and Cuba in a way that I had never heard him, or any other teacher for that matter, talk before. I can't remember his exact words. I can remember that for the first time in my life it occurred to me that all that stuff in the headlines, and on the radio, and TV had something to do with me, and that in this case it had something to do, directly, with whether I was going to go on living or not. At 17, you think you are immortal or at least in complete charge of your life. What adults do is largely irrelevant. Sitting there in Mr. Ritchie's class I saw really clearly that I was in fact mortal, that my life was in the hands of a bunch of adults I didn't even know, and that the adult I did know, the teacher, the authority figure, was scared shitless.

Thinking back on it now, as an adult myself, I think that's how Mr. Ritchie did it. I think he managed to communicate to us somehow his fear and his lack of power, his passionate concern, in a way that no other teacher ever had. That was his great gift to us, I see now, though at the time, sitting there beside R. T. smelling his starch and Lifebuoy smell, feeling him beside me in that direct absolute way in which you feel people beside you when you are 17, I only knew that what this meant was that I would never see him — R. T. — again, that we were all going to be dead before we had even had a chance to be alive.

I regard that moment in Mr. Ritchie's history class as one of the profound revelations of my life, though even as I say that and try to tell you what it was like it sounds maudlin, melodramatic, overly emotional. Personally, I am not ashamed of this. Personally, I believe that if more of us became overly emotional about the fact that a handful of people hold the power of life and death over the rest of us, things might be in a rather different state than they are today. Personally, I think history cannot be taught adequately in a way that makes it a useful science in our lives unless it is taught passionately.

However, to go on. We didn't all die, obviously, and Mr. Ritchie's classes went on. But I was changed, though at the time I didn't know how much. That year, I did a history term paper on the growing civil rights movement in the States. I began to read the newspaper and to watch TV.

That fall when I came to Queen's I joined the CUCND — Combined Universities Campaign for Nuclear Disarmament. I began to attend the meetings of various left-wing groups on the campus, including a workshop on the theory and practice of non-violence. As the years went on — and I went from undergraduate to graduate studies — I became increasingly involved in political activities. Eventually, I spent more time with my political friends than I did in classes.

In 1967 I attended my first women's meeting, held during a larger meeting of what was then called SUPA (Student Union for Peace Action), and that led me to a number of activities, ranging from disrupting the House of Commons in May 1970 over the issue of abortion legislation, to helping to found what is now Queen's Co-op Daycare.

In 1970, I finally dropped out of my graduate program in English and spent the next year traveling. I lived in communes in Saskatoon and Vancouver and eventually came back to Windsor, Ontario to be involved in a co-op bookstore, a left-wing movement within the UAW, a women's center and a number of other political activities.

Of course, some of this would have happened obviously even if Mr. Ritchie had not taught his Cuban Missile Class the way he did; some of it would have happened, I suppose, even if the Cuban Missile Crisis had itself not occurred. But not all of it. The history I have just briefly described is the history of a large segment of my generation. It is a period of our collective history which it is the fashion nowadays to refer to ironically, if not disparagingly. The media tends to present that decade in its long-hair and drug-smoking manifestations only, as if those activities were all that went on during that time, or were in fact unrelated to the political events and activities which were simultaneous with them. There is a tendency to think of the sixties as our collective adolescence and to be smug and condescending about it now that we've "grown up."

I find this attitude absurd, if not downright dangerous. It does a disservice both to adolescence, as an important period of growth for each of us, and to our shared history as a culture. It assumes, somehow, that adolescent rebellion, so-called, is not rooted in real cultural practices and attitudes which young people find painful and insulting. This is dangerous enough, given the current statistics on adolescent suicide, drug-abuse, prostitution, etc. But when we assume it collectively — it becomes suicidal. When we say that we have outgrown the passionate concerns and ideals of the sixties we are saying, I think, that passion and concern are no longer needed. Yet, acid rain, radiation, and holes in the ozone layer are killing the planet; the U.S., a country which cannot insure the safety of its female citizens either on the streets or in their own homes, continues to involve itself in the affairs of countries like Nicaragua; the hands on the doomsday clock are closer than ever to midnight.

None of this seems too far, for me, from that history class of 1962. All of it explains to some extent why I am here, and particularly why I am here as a poet.

I began writing poetry seriously in the early 1970s; I began to take myself seriously as a poet about six years later. I could not say then — and I don't suppose I could articulate very clearly now — why I chose to start writing poetry rather than leaflets, or why, now, it is my poetry (or my fiction) that claims a kind of energy and attention from me that even other forms of writing, like my column, does not. Some of that is what I have been given, I believe, but I also believe that how I use what I have been given has a great deal to do with the way in which Mr. Ritchie talked to us on that afternoon in October 1962. He talked as if it mattered; he talked as if what he did as a history teacher could change what was happening in the world; he talked as if he believed it was possible, still, perhaps, to change what was happening in the world. At least, I believe that's why he talked to us the way he did. Otherwise, why bother? For myself, I believe that in poetry and fiction we create a world which appeals to passion as much as to reason, to the emotions, to our deepest feelings about ourselves and I believe, now, more than I did when I was 17, that a passionate response is needed if we are to have any more history to teach, any more poetry to write.

That, in the end, is why I am here. Because of the Cuban Missile Crisis and Mr. Ritchie, because I believe in the power of language — of what we say to each other — to change what we have made of our history, to "save us," if you will.

If I had a credo, I suppose it would be similar to that expressed by the European art critic, essayist, historian John Berger:

> During the eighteenth and nineteenth centuries most direct protests against social injustice were in prose. They were reasoned arguments written in the belief that, given time, people would come to see reason, and that, finally, history was on the side of reason. Today this is by no means clear. The outcome is by no means guaranteed. The suffering of the present and the past is unlikely to be redeemed by a future era of universal happiness. And evil is a constant ineradicable reality. All this means that the resolution — the coming to terms with the sense to be given to life — cannot be deferred. The future cannot be trusted. The moment of truth is now. And more and more it will be poetry, rather than prose, that receives this truth. Prose is far more *trusting* than poetry; poetry speaks to the immediate wound.

However, rather than talk about poetry, I'd like to read some. Al Purdy says that any poet has only two or three great poems in them and they just go on revising. True. One of mine arose directly out of the Cuban Missile Crisis in the sense that it comes from what a history teacher taught me, during that time, to see in the world around me. Expresses the journey I have taken since:

TESTIMONIES
for Julie Cruickshank

As the cadence in an old woman's voice
becomes the line that will lead others
into the territory her people saw,
you make me see
the importance of your work, the long hours

taping these languages which only a few
of the elders speak now. "My stories are my wealth,"
one woman tells you, "all I have to give
my children," and you help create the alphabet
that takes them there. Linguistic anthropology,
the science of making language
into maps. The crazy detours
it can take you on, that story
of the parrot up in Carcross, N.W.T.,
a bird someone brought over the pass
during the gold-rush and left at the Caribou hotel
where it lived for another sixty years
entertaining customers by singing
nineteenth-century bar-room ballads
in a cockney accent. The voice of a dead miner
kept on in a brain the size of an acorn,
all the countries of his lifetime, contracted
to its bright, improbable presence
amid men who figure they've seen
just about everything now,
so that their sitting there, listening like that
becomes part of the story too,
just as I am added when I tell it,
as anyone will be, each version
a journey that carries us all along,
as the shards of poetry, carefully labelled
and carried up through layered villages
flesh out more hands
than the two that made them.

How can any of us know
what will speak for us or who
will be heard? We who are never
satisfied, eager for the evidence

no matter how it comes, slowing the car down
as we pass the accident, to see
what's pulled from the wreckage, crowding
the ones who were at the scene, the cop
or the ambulance driver, the survivors
stepping forward for their moment, blessed
by our terrible need to know everything.
Even those women we dread
sitting next to on buses or trains,
their bodies swelling with messy secrets,
the odour of complaint on their breath,
may be prophets. Whether we listen or not
won't stop them from telling
our story in their own.

Not far from where I live, a man ploughs
someone's skull up in his cornfield
and the next spring, four more, a family maybe
though no one knows even that,
their being there at all,
and longer, the only claim that's offered.
Like the farms themselves, their few rich fields
the chance deposits of a glacier.
Even the ones that I keep looking for,
wading through goldenrod to a house
where just inside the door, the trunk of old clothes
or the chair that didn't make it
to the load on back of the truck
bears witness to those smaller choices
we all have to make
about the future
and what can be wisely carried into it.

What your work brings you to, I see now,
not the past. Each site, a threshold

into this slow discovery,
the random testimony gathered
as best we can, each of us down
to essentials, as the failed are
and the dead, who bear us forward
in their fine, accurate arms.

KOKO

"Hands developed with terrible labor by apes
Hang from the sleeves of evangelists . . . ."
   — Robert Bly in "The Great Society"

Only now it is our terrible labour
(or what we thought was ours, alone)
unfurling from the root-black fingers
of an ape. Koko, the talking gorilla.
In Ameslan, her hands are muscular
and vibrant as vocal cords, name
colours and distinguish *had* and *will*,
can make a metaphor; they choose
a tailless kitten for a pet
and christen him *All-Ball*, lie
when they need to and insult their trainer
Penny dirty toilet devil, a repertoire
of over 500 words that upset
Descartes, Marx, our known,
human world. Not to mention fellow linguists
who say it's all a trick — Polly, Polly
pretty bird or Mr. Ed. They point
to her IQ score, a meagre 85,
though when they asked if she'd choose
a tree or a house for shelter
from the rain, she chose a tree
and got marked wrong.

Who says
and what
is what it comes to, though,
the sky filling up with satellites,
the cities with paper, whole stores
of greeting cards for everything
we can't spit out ourselves,
like the scratch at the back of the brain
we no longer recognize as memory.

On the TV Reagan and Gorbachev in Geneva,
though their names don't matter much,
just two more faces over shirts and ties
discussing missile size, the "nitty-gritty"
as a spokesman puts it, while
"women are more interested in peace
and things of that nature . . .
the human interest stuff."

The human interest.
Kinda like the swings in the park
across from here, how they always
squeak, day in, day out.
The guys who trim the grass
and keep the benches painted
don't even try to fix them anymore;
they know some things are like that,
stubborn as hell, no matter how much
you make an hour or what kind of government
you get. So that what we have are humans
in Oslo, Leningrad, Peking, Thunder Bay,
Denver, Cordoba and Rome pushing their kids
on swings that *squeak   squeak   squeak*

like the creaks
and farts and stutterings the body makes
to say *here* and *here* and *here.*

After living with them,
Jane Goodall found that chimpanzees
use tools, which leaves us language
as the last thing
we've got, we think,
and at the compound, Koko looking out,
a reporter tries to keep it:

"Are you an animal or a person?"

The hands coming up, almost
before he's done: *Fine animal gorilla.*
Close to the chest, showing him
familiar palm and fingers
sing *fine* caress *animal.*

■ ■ ■ ■ ■

The Politics of Everyday

Someone phoned me the other week to get my comments on the election debate. I have to admit I said, "what debate?" I could have said, "what election?" and it would have come to the same thing. Elections, I must admit, bring out the worst in me; the flippant, if not the downright cynical part of my character. When I see those party signs going up on lawns all over the city, I want to put one out front that says "Don't Vote. It Only Encourages Them."

I won't, of course. Even *saying* such a thing very often earns me a lecture on civic responsibility and democratic rights. But I like the idea, because I think it challenges some basic assumptions about the relationship between voting and politics.

The most basic of these is the assumption that voting is our most important political responsibility, that *party* politics are the most important aspect of our political life and that once we have voted for Party X or Party Y, we have done what we can for political change. It's as if politics stops once we leave the polling booth, as if once the election is over, we can get back to our ordinary lives and let whoever is elected worry about politics.

It was French philosopher Albert Camus who said, "Free election of masters does not change either the master or the slave." For me, that statement has always been a useful one. It expresses a great deal about what I feel during election time, my sense of frustration and distrust when I see how the issues that directly affect my life are used in the various party platforms. Issues that my daily experience shows me are extremely complicated become glib slogans in the mouths of politicians, become policy that they can take a stand on in a debate as if there were only two or three ways to look at the matter. "Trust me," each of them says. "I'll make things better for you."

And yet what happens? After the election things go on much as before. Polls and party expediency become the real factors that shape what changes and what doesn't change. And one of the things that doesn't change — ever — is the fact that someone else is making the important decisions that affect my life and that, on a day-to-day basis, I can do very little about it.

Or can I? If I look at politics as meaning only what happens every few years in the polling booths, then my power is very limited indeed. That is what Camus is getting at, of course. But his statement also suggests to me that there are other forms of political action and that politics itself involves a great deal more than what happens in Queen's Park or Ottawa.

The politics that matter to me are what I call "the politics of everyday." By this I mean, basically, that politics involve every aspect of our "ordinary" lives, from the food we eat to the choices we make about education or jobs.

If I look at my own life in this way, I realize that I have a particular kind of life because I am female, white, middle-class, university-educated and heterosexual. All of these attributes have a political significance. My university education, for example, gives me an advantage in the job market, but my being female ensures that I will probably earn less than a man with only a high-school diploma. It will also affect what jobs I will be considered for and what chance I will have for advancement. Being white improves my chances of a good job just as it improves my chances of being able to rent a decent apartment. Being heterosexual ensures that I am assumed to be a "fit" mother for my son.

Yet none of these "chances" or "opportunities" that affect my life so directly are accidents. They have to do with politics, with the everyday politics that we often think of as "just natural" or "the way things are."

Take education for example. It's no accident that the majority of students taking the advanced level courses at Ontario high school, courses that prepare them for university, are the sons and daughters of professional, middle-class parents, while the children of working-class or welfare parents are more likely to be in the general or basic level courses, headed for community colleges and trade schools. We often assume that everyone is working to their "natural ability," yet study after study indicates that working-class children are encouraged, by teachers and guidance counselors, to take the lower level courses *regardless of their ability*, whereas middle-class children, regardless of *their* ability are assumed to be university material. In the same way girls are encouraged to take courses which fit them for traditional "female" jobs.

We might call this the Politics of Seeing. It means that the "givens" of our culture are so deeply rooted that we accept them without question. We see the world through the eyes of our culture, without question. We accept that the doctor's kid would make a better architect than the truck-driver's kid or that girls are "naturally better" stewardesses than airline pilots as easily as we might think that blacks are "naturally" athletic. Or Orientals inscrutable. Or homosexuals sick.

For me, the politics of everyday involves the realization that none of these "givens" are "given" at all. They were created out of certain historical developments and they can be changed. They *are* changing, all the time.

But as I see it, the *source* of that change is not usually elections and political parties. The exciting political change takes place elsewhere and election issues are at best a reflection of it. Pollution in the Great Lakes, for example, becomes an election issue only because environmentalists have spent years of work on public education. They have wrought the real political change of getting us to re-think our assumptions about our place, as one species among many, in a very sensitive ecology. In the same way, legislation for day care or equal pay for women came about because feminists have worked hard — and are still working hard — to change our view of women, just as gay activists work to confront our culture's homophobia.

Such changes take place slowly and often invisibly. Sure, there are lobbies and demonstrations, but there are also long hours of talking and arguing, challenging old assumptions, learning to see the world in a new way. This is never an easy process. The journey from a group of women getting together "just to talk" to the creation of shelters for battered women, say, is a long and painful one in which *each person* changes in some very fundamental way as she looks at herself as a woman in this particular culture.

Yet these are the changes that go on, daily, in kitchens and offices and classrooms and playgrounds and coffee-shops or wherever "ordinary" people get together to discuss their "ordinary" lives. They don't stop when an election is over. They don't start just because one's been called either.

■ ■ ■ ■ ■

When Jesus Becomes More Than a Word and Enters the World of Human Beings

Green, I type the word "green" and it shows up, immediately, in amber, on my computer screen.

Green.

I look out to my garden and there, in the small square I can see from my window, green dances in a hundred shades — the milky green of the hosta lilies near the hedge and the leaves of the hedge itself, dark in places, lighter at the tips where it needs trimming. The emerald green of the basil, the blue-green of the myrtle under the pines and the pine needles, another shade of green. Tomato vines, cucumber, bean plants. It's all green and none of it is the same.

When a word comes off the page and into the world, there's no telling what it will do.

Take cripple for instance. What do you see? Tiny Tim? The grasping capitalist played by Lionel Barrymore in *It's a Wonderful Life?* The Hunchback of Notre Dame?

"I am a cripple," writes Nancy Mairs, a woman with multiple sclerosis, in an essay entitled, "On Being a Cripple." "I choose this word to name me. I choose from among several possibilities, the most common of which are 'handicapped' and 'disabled' . . . 'Cripple' seems to me a clean word, straightforward and precise. It has an honorable history, having made its first appearance in the Lindisfarne Gospel in the 10th century." She goes on to discuss her choice (which she recognizes as hers alone and not one she would apply to others in her situation), playing with words, turning them around, exploring their possibilities:

"And I certainly don't like 'handicapped' which implies that I have deliberately been put at a disadvantage, by whom I can't imagine (my God is not a Handicapper General) . . ."; or "Most remote is the euphemism 'differently abled' which partakes of the same semantic hopefulness that transformed countries from 'undeveloped' to 'under-developed,' then to 'less developed,' and finally to 'developing' nations. People have continued to starve in those countries during the shift. Some realities do not obey the dictates of language. Mine is one of them. Whatever you call me, I am still crippled."

Not everyone would agree with Mairs' word choice, of course, and that's the point — or part of the point — of this wonderful essay. It's one of a whole series of essays by Mairs called *Paintext: Deciphering a Woman's Life*. The essays range from the one I've already mentioned to essays on raising children, on feminism, on loving men — a whole range of topics. "What?" I said to myself, "Some of these don't even mention the fact that she has MS. How can that be?"

As soon as I said it, of course, I realized that I'd come to the book with all my able-bodied prejudice intact. Mairs was right. "Whatever you call me, I am still crippled." Or rather — whatever I call her, I still see only her crippledness, her disease.

Which, of course, makes me wonder how often I've done that in the past — short-changed people because I see only the wheelchair or the crutches or the hearing aid or the white cane. Agreed with them so as not to hurt their feelings (because, after all they're, well, *handicapped*). Assumed they could speak for all disabled people — the way we sometimes expect the one person of color in a room to speak for all of Africa.

Reading Mairs' essays, though, I found myself agreeing, disagreeing, laughing, arguing — all the things I want to do in any real human relationship. Reading Mairs' essays, I learned, once again, that when a word comes into the world in a human body, it is always complex, unique and mysterious.

As I've already implied, seeing Mairs as if she were only her disease is part of a larger cultural failing. Asking the one person of color to speak for everyone is one example. There are others. Suppose I refer to my neighbors as "that Portuguese family." And suppose their kids pick our roses (as kids do). Suddenly they are "those damn Portuguese kids." As if, somehow, being Portuguese had something to do with the misdemeanor.

Or lesbian. Now there's a word that narrows our perceptions somewhat. On the page it seems to be larger than life, as if it denotes beings with pink hair and horns and large neon "LS" flashing on their foreheads. In the world, though, among human beings, it's more likely to be your sister, your daughter, the lady next door, your kid's Sunday school teacher, the cashier at your bank, your family doctor. Once again, the word in the world is never simple, always unique, as close as your own skin.

All of which brings me to the furore over the Martin Scorsese film *The Last Temptation of Christ*. I haven't seen the film yet, though I intend to. I have read the book, however, many years ago, and I remember it as vividly as if I'd read it last week. And what I remember most is the figure of Jesus Christ as a real person, a person with a history, in a specific time and a specific place, a person much like you and me. A word, if you will, come off the page and into the world of human beings. The word, as some of us would say, the word made flesh.

And, as is always the case when this happens, some of us won't like the shape it takes. It would be easier, of course, if all cripples were like Tiny Tim, and all lesbians were hairy-chested monsters with buck teeth, and all blacks looked and acted like Sidney Poitier. It would be easier, too, if every interpretation of Jesus Christ made him look like the picture on the wall of my Sunday school classroom back in Princess Street United Church.

When I say "easy" I mean, I suppose, "easy to dismiss."

As long as a word means only one thing, as long as we don't have to live with it in the world, we can go on maintaining our assumptions and our prejudices. Lesbian is just a word until your daughter comes out to you. Then you have to live with her as a fellow human being in the world. Jesus Christ as that nice, sort-of-white man on the wall back at Sunday school is pretty easy to love. But what if he's the drunk, asking for quarters down near the liquor store? Or the black kid, about to throw a bomb, in Soweto? Or your next-door neighbor with the kids who steal your roses who happens to be from Portugal?

Many years ago, I happened to see Pasolini's *The Gospel According to St. Matthew,* a film based, literally word-for-word, on the Gospel. It was an amazing event. I have never been able to read St. Matthew in the same way since. And it was amazing, for me, because of how Pasolini *interpreted* the person of Jesus Christ. He was short. He was swarthy. He had thick hands and bandy legs. He was not very pretty. And he was always, always, on the move. Even the famous Sermon on the Mount was tossed over his shoulder to those who could keep up. What this did, for me, was to convey, as nothing else had ever conveyed, the energy that is at the heart of Christianity — or, as I believe now, of any spiritual view of the world.

The key word here is "interpretation." What Kazantzakis did in his novel, what Scorsese has done in the film, is to interpret what a word means to them. As such, it becomes, truly, flesh — with all its warts and sweat and genitals and lusts and fears and hopes and defeats. That, as I understand it, is what the word becoming flesh means. To live in this world, with us, as a human being.

Another friend of mine, who's been in a wheelchair for the last 10 years of his life as a quadriplegic, refers to people like me as TABS. TABS? Yeah, Temporarily Able Bodied. I like that. I like what it makes me remember about my own frailty, my own limitations. I like how it challenges me to recognize that we are all "whole" — and all "broken." None of us is complete or completely able. And it's only when we affirm that, in each of us, that we can heal each other.

Green. Cripple. Lesbian. Jesus Christ. Just words on a page. We can use them to describe. To insult. To include. To exclude. To judge. To discriminate. To praise. To hurt. To heal. But when they enter our world as flesh, then and only then do we have to live with them. Then and only then do we receive that challenge. If we want to accept it, that is.

■ ■ ■ ■ ■

The Diversity of Women's Experience

That man over there says women need to be helped into carriages and lifted over ditches and to have the best place everywhere. Nobody ever helps me into carriages or over puddles or gives me the best place — and ain't I a woman?

Look at this arm. I have ploughed and planted and gathered into barns, and no man could head me — and ain't I a woman?

I could work as much and eat as much as a man — when I could get it — and bear the lash as well! And ain't I a woman?

I have borne thirteen children, and seen most of 'em sold off to slavery, and when I cried out with my mother's grief, none but Jesus heard me. And ain't I a woman?

The speaker is Sojourner Truth, the great feminist and abolitionist who was a slave in New York until that state abolished slavery in 1827, after which she worked as a domestic servant. The speech I've quoted from was given at a women's rights convention in Akron, Ohio, in 1851. Sojourner was answering a cleric who argued that women were too weak and dependent to be given the vote.

The idea that women were delicate "ladies" who shouldn't be spoiled by politics was commonplace. Sojourner's response, however, raises the question "which women?" As a black slave, she knew that the society which thought of middle-class, white women as delicate treated black women very differently.

I have a belt around my waist and a chain passing between my legs, and I go on my hands and feet . . . the pit is very wet where I work, and the water comes over our clogs always and I have seen it up to my thighs . . . I have drawn till I have had the skin off me; the belt and chain is worse when we are in the family way . . .

This speaker is a 37-year-old working-class woman, Betty Harris, in Victorian England. Her job — which she is here describing to a parliamentary committee on working conditions — is to drag wagons of coal from the mine to the surface. It was common to use women in places too low for horses; the loads weighed from "half a hundred weight to a hundred weight and a half." The workday lasted up to 16 hours and the children of these women were left either with other family members, or in many cases alone, drugged with laudanum (an opium-based medication) to keep them quiet.

At the same time Victorian gentlemen were arguing that to allow women to vote would "make every home a hell on earth." Again, which women were they talking about?

The situation that Sojourner Truth and Betty Harris speak from has not disappeared. Class-biased and racist ideas about the role of women are still around. In the abortion debate, for example, where the rights of the unborn are a matter of much discussion. Canadians unborn that is. If it's the unborn child of a migrant laborer in California, among whom spontaneous abortions and birth defects are very high because the fields where they work are sprayed constantly with insecticides and other chemicals, we remain silent.

Women in Canada who choose abortions are called "murderers" by some. No one levels the same charge at the shareholders of American agri-business, who earn huge profits on the produce those other women harvest. And what about those of us who like to have fresh lettuce on our table every day? If we're responsible for the unborn children of Canadian women, what's our responsibility to those of migrant farm laborers?

It is important to remember, too, that Sojourner Truth's speech was made at a *women's rights* convention. Her comments were directed not only to those who opposed women's suffrage, but also to those who supported it. Sojourner had reason to suspect that people who spoke of "women's rights" might mean only certain women and she was correct in her assumption. The history of women's suffrage in the U.S. has some very unsavory aspects, especially in terms of concessions won by white women at the expense of blacks of both sexes. The same is true elsewhere, particularly in relation to working-class women.

And the same is true today. Much of the feminist theoretical work that has been done in Canada — and the U.S. — reflects the experience of white, middle-class women. This does not mean that it is "wrong" or valueless. It simply means that it is limited — and that feminists who ignore those limitations have some re-thinking to do.

The need for this re-thinking was brought home to me recently as I watched a videotape of a speech given by a black American feminist, Bell Hooks. Hooks (also known as Dr. Gloria Watkins) is a professor at Yale University and the author of two important books, *From Margin to Center* and *Ain't I A Woman*.

In a talk she gave at Concordia University in Montreal, Bell Hooks spoke about how ignoring issues of class and race have negatively affected feminist theory. While she believes that women should concern themselves primarily with feminist issues, she believes this cannot be done without an understanding that gender, race and class are "interlocking spheres of domination." For Hooks, such a view calls into question the basic feminist tenet that all women share a common experience of male domination. Or rather, it recognizes that shared experience is only part of it. We must also reorganize the diversity of experience if we are to be successful in altering the conditions that oppress women.

Hooks uses the experience of physical abuse as an example. If a white, middle-class woman and a working-class woman of color were to discuss their experience of violence, she points out, there would certainly be many similarities — as long as they stuck to issues of gender. But if they went on to analyze the situation from the point of view of class and race — in terms of sources of support, ways of changing their situation, possibilities for the future — their experience would diverge greatly. This is not to say that the experience of violence is any worse in one class or another, but simply to recognize that class (and race) are also factors in how we experience the world — and in how we want to change it.

Hooks is particularly hard on feminists who tend to see feminism as the only necessary social vision, and men as the only obstacle to women's oppression. As she points out, quite rightly in my opinion, such a view grows from white privilege and is, in fact, a denial of the reality of that privilege. It denies to women from other races and class backgrounds the right to speak of their experience, particularly when they try to point out that men are not the only obstacle to their oppression. By concentrating only on what women share, white upper-class women have denied the part they play in perpetuating class-biased and racist views. For Hooks, however, "political solidarity is different from just talking about what you share."

Listening to Hooks talk about political solidarity reminded me of a poster I used to have. It showed a black woman leaning against a fence on an inner-city street. "Class consciousness is knowing which side of the fence you're on," it said. "Class analysis is knowing who's there with you."

When I look around me, I know that I have more in common with some men than I do with some women. I'd trust a male member of the Greens further than I'd trust Margaret Thatcher any day. Nelson Mandela, Daniel Ortega, Rick Hansen, or Daniel Berrigan inspire me as much as Germaine Greer, or Madeleine Parent, or the women of Greenham Common.

The world I am working to create — for myself, for my son, for my friends, male and female — is also being created, now, by men and women who share my vision — but who come to it through their own particular experience.

Listening to Bell Hooks reminded me that I cannot always rest with the sometimes-comforting experience of exploring what I share with other white, middle-class feminists. I have a lot to learn yet and to learn it I must enter the harder, more complex regions where women's experience begins to diverge and differ. I believe such journeys are necessary in order that that imagined world may become possible and whole — for all of us.

■ ■ ■ ■ ■

Free Trade and the Survival of Our Culture

Students represent our cultural future. They'll be carrying on the tradition for which Pierre Berton, Margaret Atwood, Alice Munro, Michael Ondaatje, and others have already secured worldwide acclaim.

Or will they? To what extent will the free-trade agreement affect their chances? What is the relation between the chances of an individual writer under the free-trade agreement and the chances for survival of our culture as a whole?

Let's take a look. Let's invent an up-and-coming young writer, a woman poet, who also writes some short fiction. Let's call her Jane. Now, let's assume that Jane's career will follow the course that most literary careers — such as Atwood's, or Ondaatje's, or my own — follow in this country. Only there'll be one important difference. Jane's career will begin and develop after this country has signed a free-trade agreement with the United States.

First of all, of course, we must consider the current situation. Jane is choosing to be a writer in a country in which Canadian-owned publishers have only 20 per cent of the market, though they publish 80 per cent of the Canadian titles. A country in which less than five per cent of all screen time goes to Canadian movies, in which 77 per cent of all magazines sold are foreign, along with 85 per cent of the tapes and records. Let's remember, too, that this situation is *not* because Canadian magazines and films and songs are not *produced*, but because of the context in which they are distributed. A country which is unique in its *lack of protection* for cultural activity, the protected and expanding Australian film industry being a case in point.

Our situation is one in which our cultural market, like our other markets, is dominated by American products, partly because of the sheer size of the American cultural industry, but mainly because the Americans see it as just that — an industry. If there's a buck to be made on selling culture Americans are ready to make it — and they're very touchy about anything that stops them.

They are also almost pathologically unenthusiastic about the cultural activity in other countries. The U.S. imports very few books, feature films, music, etc. from other countries. A free-trade market will not change this attitude. This attitude, in a free-trade market, will make it even harder to distribute Canadian cultural products.

So what cultural sovereignty is the government protecting? A maximum of 20 per cent of the market share seems to be acceptable. Nothing more, nothing else.

Back to Jane. Who is being educated, let's remember, in a post-free-trade Canada. Let's also remember that the agreement is opposed by the Canadian Teachers Federation — with good reason. What happens to Canadian school systems when they face the increasing pressure of competition in a continental marketplace? Right now, the average spending per pupil in Canada is much higher than in the U.S. ($3,420 over the three years from 1983-86 as compared to $3,199 in the U.S.) In Canada, 69 per cent of that funding comes from provincial governments and only 24 per cent from local property taxation. In the U.S., state funding covers only 48 per cent of the cost, while 45 per cent comes from local taxation. In addition, that funding is more equally distributed than it is in the U.S., a fact which is reflected in pupil-teacher ratios. In Canada, the difference in this ratio between the highest-spending province and the lowest-spending province is 80 per cent. In the U.S., it's 75 per cent.

So if Jane grows up in a poor or sparsely populated part of Canada — how good an education will she get?

Let's suppose that Jane is lucky. The school she goes to has the money to provide a creative writing course and still uses Canadian textbooks in its English classes. Jane manages to write a few poems and wins a high-school competition. If she's like most writers in this country, she'll now start looking for literary magazines in which to publish.

But wait a minute. Small Canadian magazines are protected, in part, by a requirement in the Income Tax Act which states that advertisers can only claim the cost of advertising space if the magazine is printed in Canada. This section has now been repealed under the free-trade agreement. In addition, printing and typesetting have been omitted from the definition of cultural industries. Canada held on to the postal subsidy program which allows cheaper postal rates for some publications, despite tremendous American pressure. The American Publishers Association, however, thinks they will take their complaint on this issue to GATT. In the long term, this could mean the end of support programs for Canadian magazine publication.

And the end of Jane's chances of finding a sympathetic publisher for her first poems. Let's remember, too, that Jane's first book will likely be published by a small, regional publisher, like Kingston's Quarry Press, for example. One of the unique and exciting things about Canadian small-press publishing is that it recognizes *and supports* the regional character of a country's literature. And by regional I mean distinctive, not parochial, in the way that Thomas Hardy or William Faulkner are regional writers. American book publishing is organized in terms of categories and markets, dedicated to producing huge numbers of limited range material. That's why you don't see American poets like Galway Kinnell or Sharon Olds at the supermarket, though they're as relevant to you as Sidney Sheldon. You sure wouldn't see Jane Moodie either.

In addition, remember that while Article 2005, Section 1 of the free-trade agreement provides that "cultural industries are exempt from the provisions of this agreement," Section 2 states that "notwithstanding any other provision of the agreement, a Party may take measures of equivalent commercial effect in response to action that would have been inconsistent with this agreement but for paragraph 1."

In other words, if Canadian cultural policy costs Americans money they can retaliate in any area they choose. This pits poets like Jane against steel-workers or loggers or fishermen. What kind of protection is that for Canadian culture? Or Canadian workers, for that matter?

Which brings us to jobs. Jane will need one, at first, since no one gets rich from selling a few poems. She's heard that there are going to be a lot more jobs under free trade, but look again. According to Statistics Canada, in the seven-year period from 1978-85, a net growth of 849,000 jobs was entirely attributable to Canadian-owned firms. And 99 per cent of this growth was produced by small firms. Such firms are most vulnerable to takeover in a free-trade situation. Jobs with U.S. subsidiaries declined during this period.

There's more. If she's like the majority of working women — 83 per cent — Jane will be employed in the service sector. The U.S. economy is dominated by the service sector. The U.S. is a major *exporter* of services and the free-trade agreement means that those services now provided by the public sector in Canada — health care, fire protection, postal services, prisons, day care, garbage collections — will face strong competition from private, profit-making U.S. companies. In other words, while the government says free trade will not directly affect these services, it gives no guarantee that they will not be affected "indirectly" by free-market competition. Given the other patterns I have suggested it doesn't look good.

If you want to know what will happen to the quality of these services, look at how privatization affects health care in the U.S., where a three-tiered system provides care on the basis of ability to pay. Or their policy of concentrating services which provide higher profits, thereby providing *less* in the way of mundane, everyday services. Or the policy of increasing profits by cutting staff.

Already, Ontario hospitals are in crisis because of cuts in staff. Recently, Canadian writer Adele Wiseman began losing vision in her left eye. She was told that she would have to wait at least a month for a CAT scan to determine if she had a brain tumor, despite the fact that she could go blind in the interim. Wiseman continued to press for an earlier scan, which, when she got it, revealed a tumor which was then removed. Wiseman had all the resources of her status as a writer at her disposal (I read about her situation in *The Globe and Mail*.) Jane would not. Nor would you. Or me. This is the situation now. There is no indication that a free-trade agreement will improve it.

Or suppose that Jane goes into data processing, an industry which attracts a lot of women these days. The Canadian Independent Computer Services Association predicts that under free trade, 30 per cent of the industry — that's 360,000 jobs — will relocate to sites in the U.S., where wages are lower and protective legislation minimal.

Which brings us to how the free-trade agreement will affect labor legislation, trade unions and future union organizing. And why Paul Weiller, former chair of the British Columbia Labor Relations Board, called contemporary American labor law "an elegant tombstone for a dying institution."

But, you see, I'm running out of space. I'm not running out of questions. If Jane is smart, she'll ask some too. She'll note that all the trade unions, cultural groups, women's groups, poverty associations and other groups which represent ordinary people in this country are opposed to free trade while the Business Council on National Issues, whose members are mostly bank presidents and oil company executives, support it. She'll note that the current government can't even get a decent agreement on acid rain from the U.S. That it waffles on day care and abortion. That it supports a taxation program which hurts working people and lets corporations off lightly. She'll pay attention to what Reagan-type economic measures have done to British Columbia. She'll wonder how you can protect a country's poetry if you can't protect any other aspect of a peoples' life.

And then she'll ask: What's in the free-trade agreement for me?

■   ■   ■   ■   ■

Binks's Female Affirmative Action Bill

Ever heard of Susan Binks? Unless you've been reading the back pages of your newspaper very carefully, your answer is probably "no." For now, that is. But come Friday, Susan Binks is going to be a national hero.

Heroine?

Heroette?

Whatever, Susan Binks is it. She's the independent MP from Manawaka, Manitoba, who has guided the new Female Affirmative Action Bill along the twisty, tricky route to law. And she's done it almost single-handedly. When the FAAB becomes law on Friday at noon, Susan Bink's name will be on everyone's lips.

"I couldn't have done it without Joe, of course," says Ms. Binks modestly, when I talk to her over the phone. "If he hadn't been willing to take a year off work to mind the kids I couldn't possibly have championed the bill. My ordinary parliamentary duties were almost too much as it was."

Elected by an overwhelming majority in the last election, Binks was content to be a quiet backbencher until last year. That's when FAAB, which began as a private member's bill, took over her life — and Joe took over the care of their five children.

And what exactly is FAAB? That's the exciting part. FAAB, which has received almost no attention at all in the press, is going to radically change women's lives. For good.

Here's what's going to happen:

1. As of noon Friday, all women raising children on family benefits or general welfare will receive an immediate 100 per cent increase in their incomes. A woman raising two kids on a current monthly income of, say, $650 will now receive $1300 a month. This is still at or below the poverty level in some cases, but as Susan points out, "it's a start."

2. For women who want to go back to school or to work, however, FAAB's second provision is good news: under this new legislation all universities and colleges in Canada, as well as all businesses and industries employing more than 20 people, must provide full-service, on-site day care to its students or employees. In addition — and this is one of the provisions of the bill which commentators feel will cause headaches even among its supporters — all day care workers must be paid a salary

commensurate with incomes of company directors, college regents or university presidents, whichever is appropriate.

Susan has been urged countless times to drop this provision from her bill, but she's held firm.

"We're so close now," she says, "that I know it will pass. And besides, we're always saying we love children; it's a case of putting our money where our mouth is, for once."

3. Women who choose to remain at home while their children are small, but do not qualify for family benefits, will be pleased to know that FAAB provides for them as well. As of Friday, Wages for Housework, that centuries-old demand of women, will become a reality. Starting salary will be that of an MP, with similar health benefits, dental plan and vacation package.

"Women in the home," says Susan, "should earn the same as men in the House."

4. I'm most excited about this section of the bill, which has been borrowed from practices now current in Iceland. It ensures that membership in all political parties, parliamentary committees, etc. must have at least 40 per cent representation from each sex. While it's not the 50:50 breakdown radicals had been pushing for, this clause ensures that women's representation will vastly increase in the next few months — and men's will be limited to no more than 60 per cent.

"This is what happens if you're not careful, men," one disgruntled back-bencher was overheard to say. "You give women a year [International Women's Year, 1976] and the next thing you know they're taking over the country."

And that's not all. While clauses 1–4 are certainly the basis for the vast social change that the supporters of the bill envision, clauses 5–8 are even more far-reaching.

5. This provides for an immediate reassessment of our current response to domestic violence. Instead of only providing shelters for battered women, every community in Canada must now provide a halfway house for men who batter. When police are summoned to a

situation of domestic violence, they will take the man to a halfway house, where he will stay (with provision for passes to work, etc.) until assurance can be offered that he is no longer a danger to his family. Counseling will be provided in all houses.

Susan sees this as "the most logical part of the bill. After all, for years now, women and children have had to leave their homes because of the violence caused by the man. Doesn't it make more sense for him to leave?"

6. Connected to the preceding clause, Clause 6 provides for a 10 p.m. curfew for all males over 16 in all cities in Canada.

Asked if these clauses do not represent severe restrictions on freedom of movement which may be in contravention of the Charter of Rights, Susan Binks replied: "Fear of violence and rape have restricted women's movement for years. Now it's time for us to have the streets to ourselves."

Although no one in the Prime Minister's Office would comment on this section of FAAB, a source close to the Prime Minister who refused to be identified, says that special emergency provisions have been made to deal with reactions within the House when this section of the bill passes, as it undoubtedly will.

"We're going to have a whole fleet of ambulances standing by," the source said. "We expect a lot of the older MPs to have apoplexy when they find out they're going to have to defend this one in their constituency."

7. Undoubtedly the most extreme section, however, is this clause. As of noon Friday, Litton Industries, now one of the foremost producers of the guidance systems for the cruise missile, must convert 10 per cent of their production to baby carriages. And that's only a start. Work is already underway to convert the entire industry into one which would produce guidance systems to track down men who default on support payments.

"This one will never fly," a Prime Minister's Office spokesperson told reporters this morning. "It definitely infringes on freedom of movement and the right to privacy."

When asked how he thought the cruise missile, in the event of nuclear war, would affect freedom of movement, the spokesperson offered "No comment."

8. Perhaps the most ingenious part of FAAB, however, is Clause 8, the final clause. If you've been wondering how we're going to pay for all this, Clause 8 has the answer.

First of all, there will be an immediate sales tax of 50 per cent on all "skin magazines," from *Playboy* to hardcore porn. And a 50 per cent rental tax on all "adult" videos.

Military colleges, like the Royal Military College in Kingston, will be charged a substantial tariff or head-tax on all students enrolled in its programs. The tariff will be levied annually and will increase in direct relation to the number of students still enrolled in subsequent years.

"This does two things," Susan points out. "It provides money for social change and discourages military colleges from recruiting students at the same time."

Such a tariff could have far-reaching implications for military recruitment in general. So far, the Defence Department has refused to comment.

In addition to these sources of income, the National Hockey League, the Canadian Football League and both major baseball leagues will be required to donate 30 per cent of their seasonal box-office earnings to the "FAAB Kitty" as it's already being called.

"Seems fair to me," a Prime Minister's Office spokesperson said, during an uncharacteristic moment of levity. "You know the old adage. All Play and No Work Makes Jack a Jerk."

So how is Susan Binks spending her last few days of anonymity? "Mostly with my kids," she says. "Though of course I've made appointments for a haircut and a facial. I want to look my best when the spotlight's on me."

As it will be on Friday at noon.

That's Friday, April 1, of course. The group behind Susan is the Federation to Oust Outdated Laws Soon.

F.O.O.L.S.

Did I getcha?

But for a moment there, did you think it might be possible?

■ ■ ■ ■ ■

How Wise Is It To Separate Our Emotions from the Rest of Our Being?

A few years ago, I did a stint on a Canada Council Arts jury which had the task of deciding which projects, among hundreds, would receive support funding. One of the applications described a video project dealing with sexual abuse. As usual, the pros and cons of the project were discussed at length by the six jury members. I had a great deal to contribute, since I was also working at Kingston Interval House at the time, and my fellow jurists valued my opinion on the usefulness of the project. One person, however, was vigorously opposed to the application and, as the discussion became more intense, I found myself crying.

"Found myself crying" is exactly the right phrase. I didn't intend to cry; I didn't even want to cry. But cry I did. Not great, heaving sobs, mind you, but tears sufficient to be noticeable and to bring on one of those tense silences that displays of emotion of this sort often elicit.

I was mortified. Here I was trying to engage in a rational discussion about the merits of a project in which I had no direct investment, organized by people I didn't even know, and here I was weeping because someone else disagreed with me. It didn't help, either, when the project was eventually approved later in the session. Then, of course, I worried that the other jury members had felt pressured by my outburst, that I would be perceived as one of those manipulative women who gets her way by crying.

This incident came back to me recently when I read an article about how crying at the workplace can damage a woman's credibility and her career. Although there was some disagreement about isolated displays of emotion, all executives quoted in this article seem to agree that repeated expressions are detrimental. One interviewee, Pittsburgh author Paula Bern, was quoted as saying "You've got to be calloused and tough if you're a woman in power. If you can't keep your emotions under control, you shouldn't run for public office or expect to be in high-level management."

Keeping "your emotions under control." I wonder about that. What does it do to us, for example?

A few years ago, the *Whig-Standard* ran an article by Jodi Vernon about tears and some of the research connected to them. Some of the findings are very interesting. It would appear, for instance, that crying easily — or not crying at all — is learned, rather than genetic. Women *do* cry more than men, not because they are "naturally" more emotional, but because there are strong social sanctions against men expressing emotion through tears.

Yet the research indicates that tears are very healthy. Non-criers are more likely to have high blood pressure, peptic ulcers, cardiac problems, headaches and skin eruptions than people who cry more easily. In addition, researchers in one experiment studied the tears of subjects who cried when viewing a sad movie and found that they contained higher levels of protein and albumin, which are considered toxic "stress" chemicals, than the tears produced when the subjects were exposed to fresh-cut onions.

It would appear, then, that crying may be more than a psychological release. One of the reasons you feel better after a good cry could be that your tears have actually cleansed your body of toxins produced by stress. The article quotes Hans Selye, the late author of *The Stress of Life*, as saying: "We are just beginning to see that many common diseases are due largely to errors in our adaptive response to stress, rather than by direct damage by germs, poisons and other external agents."

All of this brings up important questions about how wisely — and indeed, how easily — we can really separate our emotions from the rest of our being. For me, it also means taking a hard look at what we mean when we talk about keeping our emotions "under control." Recognizing how we feel and deciding how we are going to express it appropriately is one thing. Disregarding or denying how we feel in order to appear in control is another. Too often, we confuse the two. Studies of violent, abusive men, for example, show that they are often incapable of recognizing and expressing such feelings as fear, sadness or vulnerability. But that does not mean these feelings are "under control"; rather, it means that they often get expressed as anger. Or in my own case, if I had realized that, given my work situation, the discussion of the video project was likely to be stressful, I might have been able to express that in words and not suddenly "found myself" crying.

And how much can we really separate what we "feel" from what we "think?" To what extent is our culture's emphasis on rationality the result of a truly *irrational* fear of emotion and its place in any decision-making process? What's wrong with emotions being part of decisions anyway?

I think it's important to look critically at where this attempt to separate rationality from emotion has got us. At present, we in Kingston, Ontario live in one of the most highly polluted areas in North America, the Windsor-Montreal corridor. We live in a province whose government, according to a recent news report, does not have any idea how much of its remaining timber the forest industry can safely cut without doing even more damage to the ecology. We live on a planet where $900-billion is spent annually on arms, while 40,000 children die every day, most of them from starvation.

I would argue that this state of affairs has grown out of emotions such as fear, greed and anger. I would also argue that it is largely the result of decisions made by people who consider themselves rational human beings whose ability to make such decisions is unclouded by "dangerous" emotions.

If that's the case, I'd say we need a lot more tears in the workplace.

■ ■ ■ ■ ■

Rape: How the Law Makes Victims Guilty

A few years ago I was involved in a women's art festival in Kingston that was to raise money for various feminist organizations, one of which was the Sexual Assault Crisis Center. I took a poster advertising the event to a nearby store and asked the owner if I could put it up. He refused to allow it.

"I don't think we need a crisis center," he said. "If a woman acts right, she doesn't need to worry. Nice girls don't get raped."

My neighborhood grocer is not alone in his opinion, which, indeed is shared in one way or another by almost everyone. It is part of the "accepted wisdom" of our culture. It is also enshrined in our law.

I'm talking about the old practice of questioning rape victims in court about past sexual history. Until quite recently, a victim's sexual history was considered relevant evidence in determining whether or not she had "really" been raped. Laws restricting such evidence are now in place, but those laws are being challenged as unconstitutional and as "unfairly affecting the accused's rights."

Recently, a decision by the Ontario Court of Appeal ruled, three to two, that these laws *are* constitutional. This is only a minor victory for women, however. For one thing, similar cases are now before the Supreme Court, which means that the present restrictions could still be challenged. As well, the whole issue of sexual history raises grave questions about how our culture views women's experience and about what it assumes is men's responsibility.

Historically, the issue of sexual history was related to the issue of a particular witness's credibility or character. In rape trials, it was assumed that the testimony of an "unchaste woman," like that of, say, an ex-con in another situation, could not be believed. It was also assumed that the fact that a woman had had sexual relations with other men meant that she was the sort of *character* who would consent to anything. In other words, in cases where a woman had previous sexual experience, there was often "no such thing" as rape.

Although current laws now restrict the use of such evidence, there are exceptions to these restrictions in three specific areas. Sexual history evidence is admissible: 1) when it is used to refute evidence put forward *by the woman* about her own sexual history; 2) when it is considered relevant to a dispute about the identity of the accused (i.e. someone else committed the rape, though the accused may have been present); and 3) when her sexual activity on the occasion in question could be construed as consent on the part of the accused (i.e. she had sex with someone else on the same occasion, so the accused assumed she consented to him).

In the various challenges being put forward, these exceptions are seen as *too* restrictive and the law itself is seen as violating the right to a fair trial guaranteed by the Charter of Rights and Freedoms.

For me, though, the issue confronting us is not primarily a legal one. In fact, I don't think that it can even be resolved as a legal issue. Laws, after all, are made in a specific social context and the laws around rape have to do with how women are perceived, how women are heard and whether women are believed. When I talked to lawyer Sheila McIntyre, in an attempt to find my way through the legal maze, we touched on those wider issues as well.

We began by asking questions. What do the current exceptions to the restrictions on sexual history say about how rape is perceived in our society?

Let's look at the "mistaken identity" exception first. First of all, what sort of situation is being assumed? A party? A gang-rape? Group sex? And why, in these situations, is the woman's sexual history relevant and not, say, her ability (or inability) to identify her assailant correctly out of a crowd or gang of possible assailants? And, even if she has made a mistake, why is the issue of the accused's presence in such a situation, his being, in a sense, *accessory* to rape never even raised?

The situation of "presumed consent" also calls up images of group sex situations in which, since a woman has had sex with two men, say, the accused can be seen as having a reason to assume she consented to him. But why? Why do we never challenge the basis of *that* assumption? Does the fact that a woman consents to two men *necessarily mean* that she'll consent to anyone else? How far have we really come from the idea that "that sort of woman" *deserves* to be raped and that a man shouldn't have to go to jail over a "tramp"?

These exceptions to the restrictions on sexual history are based on the assumption that the rights of the accused need further protection than that already provided by law. They also assume that it is common for women to lie in accusing men of rape and that rape by a stranger or a group of strangers is a frequent occurrence.

Yet according to Julie Darke of the Sexual Assault Crisis Center, studies based on police files indicate that the rate of false accusations of rape is two per cent, the same rate as for other violent crimes. There is also overwhelming evidence that, in 75 per cent of all cases, the woman will know her rapist at least by sight and in 50 per cent of all cases, he will be someone she knows well, an ex-partner or a "friend." In the case of sexual assault on children, the assailant is known to the child in 80 per cent of the cases.

Julie also pointed out that only one in 10 cases of rape are ever reported to the police in the first place. Most women turn to crisis centers for supportive counseling, but few want to face the courts. This is because they are aware of how difficult the process is, because they fear that friends, co-workers and relatives will find out *and because they fear that they will be blamed for what has happened.* This fear is a real one. The hard fact is that women *are* blamed for crimes committed against us. Just as the battered wife is asked what she did to "deserve it" the issue of sexual history assumes that something in the woman's past makes her "fair game" for a rape or at least unworthy of society's protection against it.

This attitude is also evident in a recent attempt by the Edmonton City Council to make women who wear "suggestive clothing" guilty of sexual harassment. No one asks, suggestive of what? To whom? And until such questions are asked, loudly and frequently, we are left with the stereotype of men as over-sexed, slobbering idiots who can't control their animal impulses and women as quasi-angelic guardians of some obscure sexual morality.

Or is it "sexual morality" at all? Part of the problem I have with the issue of sexual history and rape is that it plays into the whole myth that rape is essentially a sexual act. We're all familiar with those scenarios in movies and TV shows where a woman starts out protesting a man's sexual advances and ends up liking them. It's the basis for a lot of pornography also, like the idea that women "like to tease" or that "no really means yes."

But what if the scenario were one in which someone protested being hit over the head with a baseball bat and ended up liking it? Unimaginable, right? Rape is no less violent and no less a crime. The fact that it is violence involving sexual organs does not change this. In fact, we might want to ask why men choose to use their bodies against women in such a violent manner.

The reality of women's experience is that *at least* 82 per cent of us will be sexually assaulted at some point in our lives. This can be anything from unwanted touching to violence, mutilation and death. In addition, most women experience occasional sexual pressure of one form or another, even from men they like. In a society where men hold enormous economic and emotional power over women, "giving in" is often easier than fighting about it or having to say "no" over and over again. In many women's eyes, this scenario is a lot more common than the romantic seductions we see in the movies. In other words, sexual relationships in our society cannot be separated from other aspects of the relationship between men and women.

As I see it, our rape laws still do not reflect this relationship accurately. In the process of changing them, we are going to have to ask a lot of questions about the nature of men's attitudes toward women. These are not moral or legal questions so much as political questions, in the widest possible sense. They are questions about how we are going to create a community where women and men can live together in trust and without fear. Decisions like that of the Ontario

Court of Appeals are only a very small beginning. We all have a lot of work to do.

■ ■ ■ ■ ■

Away from Familiar Ground: Two Stories of Choices Made in Alien Worlds

"The universe," said American poet Muriel Rukeyser, "is made of stories, not of atoms." In that spirit, I have two to tell.

There was once a young woman named Karen. After she graduated from university she worked, for a while, at a series of not very challenging jobs. Then she got a break — a position with an excellent future in the area for which she'd been trained. Everyone was glad for her; her close friends had worried a little about Karen. Sometimes she seemed "too" emotional, particularly in the anger she expressed towards her father and older brother, though her friends could see no real reason for her attitude.

Karen moved to a new city and soon her friends were getting excited phone calls about the friends she was making, how much she was enjoying her job. But after a few months, the excitement began to change to desperation. Karen's anger at her family began to increase, though she was now living some distance from them. Finally, it all came out. Karen was remembering that she was an incest survivor, that her older brother had repeatedly tried to rape her when she was a young adolescent.

Though it was difficult at first, Karen began to get help from a counselor. She read several books about incest; she talked openly to her friends about how she was feeling. Once again, she was getting her life together. Soon, she began to talk about a man she was falling in love with.

A few months later Karen was pregnant. Although the pregnancy was unplanned, she wanted the baby and began discussing working motherhood, its pros and cons, with friends who had children. She was worried, though, about the baby's father — he was withdrawing, telling Karen she was on her own. Confused, Karen persuaded him to visit a counselor with her and in the course of these sessions it came out that he, too, was an incest survivor. The idea of having a baby terrified him. He did not feel he was ready to be an active father, nor could he promise Karen any support. She was on her own.

Faced with the prospect of raising a child alone, in a relatively new city, having just settled into a new job, Karen began to re-think her decision. Learning of her lover's incest experience brought back her own pain and anger. Was she ready to have a child? Could she be the kind of parent she truly wanted to be? For weeks, Karen talked to her counselor, to her friends, to herself, trying to decide what to do.

In the end she chose, very reluctantly, to have an abortion and made an appointment at a free-standing clinic in a nearby city. When she arrived, the clinic was surrounded by demonstrators who called her names and thrust pamphlets into her hands as she entered the clinic.

Several months later, Karen is still feeling shaky, still feeling the pain of a decision which was, she believes, the "right" decision, but not an easy one. At her urging, her lover is seeing a counselor and the two have agreed not to see each other until he has dealt with some of his own confusions.

That's one story. Here's another, shorter one. Melissa and Jennifer are a lesbian couple who have been together for over 20 years. Both are professionals, successful in their respective fields. Four years ago they had a baby by alternate insemination, arranged by a doctor. Last year they decided they wanted a second child and were dismayed to find that their doctor was no longer willing to arrange it. Luckily for them, they found, through a third party, another donor and they now have a healthy baby girl. Melissa chose to be the birth mother to both children, but Jennifer does more than half of the child care. The children call both women "Mommy" and the four-year-old even boasts proudly to his friends that he has two mommies where most people only have one.

For me, both these stories are stories about choice. And, of course, they are not "just" stories. They are actual happenings in the lives of some of my friends.

Being friends with Karen and Melissa and Jennifer is not always easy for me. As a woman in a long-standing, monogamous relationship, I find Karen's world very alien; I don't know anything about the context in which she made the choice she did about her baby. I was the same age as she is now — and at the same point in my career — when I decided to have my son. Things have gone well for me; I have trouble seeing why they wouldn't go well for her. I can "know," intellectually, about the pain and anger of being an incest survivor, but I can't feel its weight as a factor in her life, in her choices.

As a heterosexual, I am cut off, in many ways, from the life that Melissa and Jennifer live. I can't imagine raising two kids, as lesbian parents, in this culture. Why would they want to? How do they deal with the attacks they must experience? How can they be happy? How will their kids "turn out"?

Often, my love for Karen and Melissa and Jennifer is colored by loss. Loss of familiar ground, shared experiences. Sometimes, that sense of loss translates itself into anger at their "other-ness," their "wrong-headed" choices. When I feel this anger, I sometimes wish for a system of absolutes, a transcendent world view that would put my friends "out there," on the "other side" and protect me from the loss I feel. Yet could it ever protect me from all that I feel for them, that tangle of emotions, complex as the details of their particular life-stories? Or would a worldview that shut them out be an expression of the fact that I don't have to feel that complexity?

If I shut them out, I shut out the challenges they offer. I wouldn't get to look at the world through their eyes. When people talk about "lesbian mothers" in a derogatory manner, I would simply have words in my head — not Melissa's face as she bends down to kiss her son or Jennifer's voice trying to talk over the racket of two kids in the background. When I read about a demonstration outside an abortion clinic, I could turn the page to other news. I wouldn't have to remember Karen's face, collapsing into tears, or how her shoulders shook when I held her. I wouldn't have to hear her voice over the telephone these days, the crying barely contained, as she talks about wanting another baby someday.

For me, living in the full freedom — and absolute responsibility — of our own choices is a little like learning to ride a bicycle (and a whole lot harder, obviously). It's a matter of balance. You learn to make everything work together as part of a whole — your body, its strengths and its limitations; the strengths and limitations of the type of bicycle you've chosen; the information your senses give you; your knowledge of everything from traffic rules to road conditions. A mistake can kill you. But you're able to move at your own speed, using your own strength. And you can go just about anywhere.

Loving Karen and Melissa and Jennifer feels a bit like the moment, years ago, when I let go of my son's bike and he wobbled off, alone, independent and free. It scared me silly. Maybe he'd fall (he did). Maybe he'd be as careless as I and get hit by a car, as I had been (he hasn't, yet). I could, of course, protect him from all this by a strict system of rules, coercion and punishment. In doing so, I might protect myself from the loss that his independence creates.

In doing so, I would forfeit the world he discovers out there, alone, and brings back to share with me. I would deny him his integrity as another human being, living in the world with me. I would also deny my ideal of parenting as one in which the parent empowers, rather than overpowers, the child.

Yet this model of parent as ultimate authority has a long history in our culture. It's a model we tend to use for controlling each other's behavior, even as adults. But I want to be in the world with others in a different way, as I try to be with my son. I want to honor their choices, which grow from the unique complexities of their lives, from the stories only they can tell. My obligation as a fellow citizen is to ensure, when necessary, that they get the chance to live their stories. Their integrity and my own — politically and spiritually — depends on it.

■ ■ ■ ■ ■

Pornography and Ways of Dealing with It

Sheila McIntyre and I meet over coffee to talk about pornography leg-islation. She's a feminist lawyer; I'm a feminist writer. We're both tired of "soft-core" depictions of female sexuality that show us as passive, and we're angered by hard-core porn where women appear to enjoy rape, mutilation, and violence. We know these depictions lie. We also know that they're part of a continuum — from TV ads to snuff films — in which women are trivialized, degraded, and brutalized for the "entertainment" of the viewer who is always assumed to be male. Because there are few alternative views of women widely available in our culture, these depictions also serve to reinforce negative attitudes toward us.

Media portrayals of women are the expressions of a society which devalues us in the work place, in education and in legislation, and in which there has been little opportunity for women to tell our stories. We both see dealing with pornography as one way of confronting some of these other issues.

Neither of us support current legislation in the Criminal Code or the proposed amendments to it. The main problem with criminal leg-islation is that it's up to the police to decide whether to prosecute and then the state, in the form of Crown lawyers, to carry through with it. As Sheila says, this takes the action "completely out of the hands of anyone damaged by pornography." The other problem is that pornog-raphy is still defined as a *moral* offence, which leaves us open to the kind of censorship that goes on when books like Margaret Laurence's *The Diviners* are removed from high-school curriculums.

There are other forms of legislation, however. Sheila would like to see us use human rights legislation, which would mean re-defining it "not as morally offensive, but as a means of discriminating against women." The resulting action "would be a *civil* action, like a negligence suit, so that the individual victim initiates." This would mean that *women* would get to tell their stories about the making of pornography in the courtroom: "A real woman claiming to be really injured is there for you to see and hear, instead of the police."

I want women to have an opportunity to tell their stories, but doing this in a courtroom even in a civil action, still means that the context is punitive. And what is being punished is not necessarily a violent act against a woman but the *depiction* of a violent act. This is still a form of censorship which could have serious implications.

Sheila doesn't see it that way. "The suit doesn't happen before the printing, though a couple of successful suits might alter what people print. But so does the market. That doesn't worry me. The suit can't be brought until some woman's been forced to make the pictures; that's already happened and then I don't think it should lie in any feminist's mouth to say 'let's protect the pictures.' A woman has been raped to make them. We don't want the pictures circulating of a woman's rape for profit. No feminist should support that, ever. I'm absolute on that."

True. But if a woman has been raped to make the picture, why not use existing legislation to get a conviction of rape? Depictions of violent acts do not necessarily mean that the acts happened in reality. What sort of connections are we making here between pictures and/or words and actual experience? These questions lead us to the issue of causal links between violent pornography and violence against women. Can we be sure that pornographic depictions of certain acts cause men to commit them? Sheila feels certain that they at least help to shape and reinforce negative attitudes. And she points out that after only six deaths by cyanide-poisoned Tylenol, the entire industry has sealed containers. "Even though it was one crazy person, probably, it changed the whole industry. We act on material risks all the time. The woman whose husband brings home a porn magazine and says 'do this' and is beaten into it should have a suit."

I agree. Her husband should be charged with rape and assault. I believe that the man who brings home pornographic pictures and forces his wife to perform degrading acts already sees the world through misogynist eyes. The pictures *confirm* his view, certainly, but I think the connections between what he sees and what he does are extremely complex. To me, suing the pornographer is like saying that J.D. Salinger should be sued because Mark David Chapman had a copy of *The Catcher in the Rye* with him when he shot John Lennon.

Sheila suggests another way of looking at this by comparing the producers of pornography to the producers of defective cars. "We sue for damages; we get the car recalled. The producers of pornography, from the photographers through to the publishers and distributors, have to take responsibility for their product. If their product injures someone, as producers they're liable."

This is where I *really* disagree. I don't think words and pictures are the same as automobiles.

But Sheila questions whether pornography is "just an idea. One buys it to be aroused; it's sex when it's used to make sex. When it's used to masturbate with, then it isn't an idea."

To me this blurs the lines between reality and *representations* of reality in a dangerous way. I'm nervous about how the legislative route seems to make light of the extent to which our experience affects our interpretation of what we see. Suppose I write a series of poems about domestic violence, some of which are very descriptive. Someone could interpret these poems as condoning violence against women. Suppose he beats his wife. Suppose she decides to take me to court.

Now I know, as Sheila points out, that the wife still has to prove there's a connection. "People may think this is hogwash," she says, "but at least the argument doesn't get foreclosed from the start because of what might get caught up in it."

But it's exactly "what might get caught up in it" that makes me distrust legislation. I see my job as a writer as trying to give expression to as much human experience as I can. Since I am a woman, much of this experience will be female and for that reason a lot of it will be previously *unexpressed* experience. When I look at what other women artists are doing, I know that a lot of what we have to say is going to be disturbing, frightening, ambiguous and therefore open to many interpretations. But I think we need to be able to say it, so that other women can look at it and decide how it relates to their own lives. I know that the fear of being sued, self-censorship, would prevent some of that from happening.

We come back again and again to the opportunity for women to tell their stories.

Sheila says, "I see myself as a feminist lawyer working inside an overwhelmingly male-tilted system. And I see this kind of legal remedy as women drafting the law, litigating it, women's voices finally being heard in court, telling it their way. I stay ambivalently in this profession because I don't think women and the disadvantaged people most hurt by law can afford to write it off. I think we have to take legal tools and try to put women's voices into them and then put women into the courtroom to tell their stories."

And I see myself as a feminist writer whose job it is to explore what our culture has previously silenced. For 2,000 years, women's stories have not been heard. I trust the power of these stories eventually to speak more strongly than pornography's lies. I think we've got to be very, very careful about supporting any legislation that could affect these explorations when they're only just beginning. I also think there are other ways of dealing with pornography besides restrictive legislation.

Sheila and I talked for over three hours, until the coffee pot was long empty and we both had to get on to other things. We didn't come to any final agreement, but we did realize we had begun a conversation that will continue for a long time yet. We hope other women will begin it, too.

■ ■ ■ ■ ■

Thoughts on the Vulnerability of Humans, Prompted by a Trip to Emergency

A few weeks ago my son was hurt at school. He's okay now, and it turned out that his injuries were minor. But I had to live through those blurred hours that every parent dreads: that eternity between the phone call that said, "There's been an accident," and the doctor at emergency who finally told me, "He's okay; you can go home now."

"That clench in the gut," Margaret Laurence calls it, "at the thought of anything happening to one of our kids."

As my son gets older, though, I am aware of a difference. I am aware that my son is learning, very quickly, to make light of his injuries, so that even a few days after his last accident, he acted as if nothing much had happened. My worry for his safety — or his health — was just silly, old motherish nonsense.

Now some of this, of course, is a necessary and healthy part of growing up. We can't always have our mothers there to remind us to take our Vitamin C and watch where we're going; we need to shrug our mothers off a bit so we can explore the world for ourselves.

It's not that that I'm worried about, though. It's something else. It's the sense that, in this culture at least, part of a boy's growing up involves his becoming invulnerable. Tough. Able to take it. Among my son and his peers, there is increasing concern and discussion about "bullies," about potential fights in which someone might really get hurt. In fact, how to deal with peer violence seems to be part of adolescence, as "natural" as the alarming rate of growth that only teenage boys are able to achieve. When I took part in a recent discussion about raising sons at International Women's Day, this topic was the one most women raised. Fighting. Having to win. Having to be tough.

It's not surprising, of course, given that we live in a culture where "being a man" too often involves learning how to act like Clint Eastwood, even if you feel like Sissy Spacek inside. In fact, it seems to me that "being a man" in this culture involves denying that you have any "Sissy Spacek feelings" at all. That's the kind of stuff that gets left up to women to experience and deal with.

And because male experience has dominated our idea of what *human* is, our view of ourselves as a culture often includes this idea that we have to be invulnerable, that we have to "win."

Such a cultural self-image expresses itself in many ways. In the way we talk about disease for example — "beating" cancer, "overcoming" heart disease, "fighting" the common cold. Such a language gives little space to talk about the fact that we are relatively fragile organisms, that we have to take care of ourselves, that we are mortal. Instead, we put the emphasis only on finding cures, while those with terminal illnesses are shunted away, out of sight. We focus on replacing parts of the body with new organs, as if it was a machine, and talk very little about living a life that would protect that body we've already got.

We never take the time to ask ourselves what can be learned from those who are handicapped or injured or dying of cancer. What do they have to teach us about accepting limitation, learning to live with what cannot be changed or denied? We deny to ourselves the opportunity of learning from the dying a great deal about how to live.

Our denial of limitation and vulnerability affects us on an emotional and spiritual level as well. In discussions of serious matters like abortion, for example, we prefer the simple and the absolute: I'm right, you're wrong. We want easy answers — we believe there *are* easy answers.

Yet we hardly ever ask any questions. It's easier to hate homosexuals, for example, than to examine our own sexual uncertainty, our confusing and conflicting fears and desires. We hardly ever admit to our own fear, or confusion, or uncertainty. To do so would open us to admitting that we're no different from the next person doing what seems best to make sense out of the muddle of living. It would also open us to admitting that we can't decide for other people — we can't legislate — how to resolve that muddle. We'd have to trust them, as we trust ourselves.

As a culture we've accepted the notion that spiritual wholeness means closing ourselves off to "sin," to that which is confusing, or different, or in conflict with what we believe. Spiritual wholeness then becomes a suit of armor that closes us off from the world, rather than an inner power that opens us to all our possibilities.

As a culture, ours is only one — and a fairly recent one — among many. Unfortunately, ours is also a very powerful culture. "Winning" our dominant place on the planet has meant that we do not ask questions of those we conquer. It's easier to assume that native peoples, or "Third World" cultures are "backward" and "uncivilized" rather than ask what we can learn from them, where they have gained the power to continue against all our attempts to destroy them.

To anyone who wants to explore this aspect of our cultural invulnerability further, I recommend Hugh Brody's books. Brody is an anthropologist who has lived with and written about the native people of the north for almost 20 years. In his latest book, *Living Artic*, he says, "I write about the far north in the belief that we can best discover who we are by going to what we think of as the margins of our world. Faced with societies and lands that question our everyday assumptions and challenge our preconceptions, it is possible to discover both the importance of others and truths about ourselves."

And finally, as a species we are only another one among thousands — and *just* another one at that. No matter how ferociously we place ourselves at the top of the hierarchy of plants, insects, birds and other animals, we cannot escape from the fact that we must live on this very small planet with them, that our survival cannot be separated from theirs. By denying that we are a vulnerable species, much like any other, we have denied this connection. We have become the sort of people who refer to any piece of the earth that isn't covered with a freeway or a condo as "waste" land, as if our purposes and our needs were the only ones.

So where does it get us, all this posturing and denial? In my son's case, it'll probably mean a few more trips to emergency before he catches on that he's not made of plastic. For many of the adult males he sees around him, it may mean a lot of emotional pain and hard work before they accept that they don't have to know all the answers, win all the arguments, control all the situations they're in. It's okay to be afraid or confused or sad. Among individuals, these small struggles and changes take place daily and very slowly.

As a culture, though, the situation is much more difficult. My daily read through the newspapers, including the letters to the editor, does not always leave me feeling very optimistic. There seem to be a lot of people with answers out there — who haven't even asked any questions yet. Or not enough questions, anyway.

As a species, our situation is already critical. If we don't start accepting our limitations, our vulnerability, our denial, will kill us all. Literally. It's as "simple" as that.

■ ■ ■ ■ ■

Meaning What We Say

"Come, we shall have some fun now!" thought Alice. "I'm glad they've begun asking riddles — I believe I can guess that," she added out loud.

"Do you mean that you think you can find out the answer to it?" said the March Hare.

"Exactly so," said Alice.

"Then you should say what you mean," the March Hare went on.

"I do," Alice hastily replied, "at least — at least I mean what I say — that's the same thing, you know."

"Not exactly the same thing a bit!" cried the Hatter. "Why, you might just as well say that 'I see what I eat' is the same thing as 'I eat what I see.'"

"You might just as well say," added the March Hare, "that 'I like what I get' is the same thing as 'I get what I like.' "

— Lewis Carroll

The March Hare and the Mad Hatter are right, of course. Saying what we mean — and meaning what we say — is an extremely complex business. We don't need to go to Wonderland to find out how complex, though. A quick trip through any newspaper, published any day in this country, will suffice.

Take the recent reporting of the discussion *within* the United Church about ordaining gays and lesbians.

"Recommendation to ordain homosexuals threatens to split church," most headlines read.

What? How can somebody's wanting to be ordained as a minister within a church threaten to split it? What's going on here?

What's going on is that the recommendation about ordaining homosexuals gave rise to strong opposition from some church members. They've threatened to leave if it's accepted.

So how come the headlines didn't read, "Homophobia and bigotry threaten to split church?" That's what we really mean to say, isn't it?

Or is it? Maybe we are saying what we mean when we locate the cause of the split with "them." "Those homosexuals." It's certainly easier that way. Saves a lot of trouble on *our* part.

"We heterosexuals," obviously, since "we" are always "we" and "they" are always "they." If we can just keep that straight (pun intended) we don't have to examine our own bigotry.

I mean, look at that Svend Robinson fellow. Not only does he admit to being one of "them," he also says that there are more of "them" in the government.

"Flaunting his homosexuality," one columnist called it.

Funny, when someone vandalized Robinson's office after his announcement, there were no headlines reading, "Vandals flaunt heterosexuality in Burnaby."

Instead we had a lot of MPs reacting angrily to the possibility that some of "us" might be "them." Talk about flaunting! Alberta Tory Jim Hawkes accused Robinson of "casting aspersions." Nova Scotia Tory Pat Nowland worried about being "tarred with the same brush." No one mentioned the fact that being thought homosexual is only a problem if you're a bigot in the first place.

"Curiouser and curiouser," says Alice.

Curious, too, is William Vander Zalm's remark that his province was being "blackmailed" by the Supreme Court decision on abortion. He does not, of course, consider his decision to refuse public funding of abortions "blackmail."

Oh, my, no. Even after the British Columbia Supreme Court struck down these regulations, Vander Zalm remarked, "We're not changing our policy. We're not having the taxpayers pay for abortions on demand."

Ah, the taxpayer. How convenient. Are there no taxpayers in British Columbia who might disagree with Vander Zalm? According to several polls, there are. And isn't it odd that Vander Zalm never once invoked that beleaguered figure when the Socreds were spending and overspending millions on Expo?

A man who loves children, though, Bill Vander Zalm. That's why his government turned down a request from the Vancouver School Board for $200,000 to feed the 500-700 school children who come to school hungry every morning.

Of course, the school board can have the money if it turns the names of the children over to the Ministry of Social Services. But school teachers and principals are unwilling to do this because they fear that the ministry would begin investigating to see if there is parental neglect. In Vander Zalm land this is called "upholding the family" I believe. You know, keeping it from the "embarrassment" of social assistance. "Saving the taxpayer," right?

We won't mention the cutbacks in social services that have caused the problem in the first place, of course. And we won't talk about how poor people are also taxpayers.

Just like women who want abortions.

Curiouser and curiouser indeed.

And not just in British Columbia either. In Ontario, a Supreme Court judge has ruled that a lesbian couple represents a "distinct class" and cannot have the same rights as heterosexual couples. His ruling came in response to a lesbian couple's request for family coverage under the Ontario Hospitalization Insurance Plan.

The judge's logic is a little hard to follow, but hold on, I'll try. "Heterosexual couples procreate and raise children," he says. True enough, they do. Though I also know several lesbian couples who have had children via alternate insemination. I know many others who are raising children from previous marriages.

However, the judge goes on, "they [heterosexual couples] have legal obligations for support for their children." Yes, they do. But so do gay parents, don't they? As I understand it, homosexuals are only a "problem" when they want something. When they are *obligated* to do something, they're treated just like any other citizen. I'll bet a homosexual parent would be charged with neglect just as fast as a heterosexual parent. Faster, probably.

Our judge, however, seems to think not. "A same-sex parent does not and cannot have these obligations," he says. The couple in question have been together nine years. Meanwhile, the province is full of absentee fathers who flaunt their heterosexuality by never paying a dime of support to their families.

Legal logic, I guess. You figure it out.

Got it? Now try this one. You know those nuclear-powered subs the government wants to run under Arctic ice to "protect" our sovereignty? They're going to cost us between $12 and $14-billion. No one says a word about the poor taxpayer, of course. And it's "protecting" our sovereignty, not flaunting it.

Just like "a government spends what it earns" means the same as "a government earns what it spends."

Welcome to Wonderland, folks! Have a nice stay.

■ ■ ■ ■ ■

Humans and Other Animals

There's a poem by Earle Birney called "The Bear on the Delhi Road," in which he describes seeing a huge Himalayan bear being brought down from the mountains by two "men of Kashmir." The men have captured the bear, not to kill him, but "simply to teach him to dance." To become a dancing bear, in the great markets of Delhi where his owners will earn a living from his performances.

Birney talks about the work it takes for these trainers to wear from the bear's "shaggy body the tranced / wish forever to stay / only an ambling bear / four-footed in berries." And the poem ends by widening that picture of this one bear into a larger image of our relationship to many other animals:

> It is not easy to free
> myth from reality
> or rear this fellow up
> to lurch — lurch with them
> in the tranced dancing of men.

Birney's poem came to mind when I saw Klass Act recently at the local shopping center. Klass Act, an outfit from Ohio, offered several lionesses performing tricks in a small cage in the parking lot. And inside, another cage held lion and tiger cubs — cute little fellas; you could have your kid's (or your own) picture taken with them.

I find the appearance of Klass Act, like Birney's bear on the Delhi road, disturbing. Seeing those lionesses in that tiny cage and those cubs being picked up for endless photographic sessions gave me that sick feeling that animal acts in the circus often give me — or the appearance of wild animals at a zoo.

I am not talking here about how "well" or how "cruelly" the

animals are treated, though that is an important issue. The Klass Act animals had the bored, listless look that the big cats often have when seen through bars. The cubs were even more listless and I couldn't help wondering how they had been rendered "safe" for close-up photos with young children. Still, we are talking about animals born and raised in captivity. Given that, to talk about the specific "cruelty" of Klass Act is to single out one rather tawdry example from a long list. If Klass Act is where we "end up," it is, as far as I'm concerned, different only in degree from the zoo or the circus. Once we have decided, as a species, that other animals can be caged and trained for our entertainment, we have made a decision as well about our relationship to those other animals. It's that relationship I want to explore.

Let me start by saying that I think the relationship between our species and other animals is a very complex one. I think, too, that there is a difference between our relationship to lions and tigers and our relationship to house cats, dogs and horses. For those who want to explore some of the complexities of the latter relationship, I recommend Vicki Hearne's book *Adam's Task* as one particularly challenging viewpoint.

I also believe that the relationship between humans and other animals varies from culture to culture. I've talked before about the work of Hugh Brody, an anthropologist who has lived for many years among the hunting tribes of the Canadian North. In his latest work — *Living Arctic* — Brody explores the complex relationship between these hunters and the animals they hunt. He recognizes that in all these cultures, this relationship is seen as spiritual as well as practical. It is a relationship of dependence, primarily, because the hunter depends on the animal for survival. "Dependence," Brody points out, "entails vulnerability. The relationship between the hunter and the hunted, therefore, has a certain equality. Ultimately, no one can be superior to that upon which he depends."

This spiritual complexity is evident in native literature, in their religious views, and in the reliance of some peoples (the Athapascan and the Algonquian, for example) on dreams to guide them to the

right hunting spots. The sense of interdependency, which is at the center of this relationship with other animals, also accounts for the fact
that these peoples kill only what they need and, in doing so, do not
usually deplete the species.

Brody also recognizes the argument often put forward by biologists that northern hunters' belief systems may only take into account
one part of a species' cycle and that they may engage in ecologically
dangerous practices. But he envisages a situation of "northern hunters
and white biologists sitting down together, agreeing about wildlife
problems and discovering ways in which these can be ameliorated."
Brody also believes that Southern attitudes about meat diets and about
hunting in general have fueled animal-rights campaigns which do not
look at the full complexity of these relationships.

Another person who has written extensively about the meaning
of our relationship to other animals is John Berger. Berger is an art
critic, novelist, and scriptwriter who is best known for a book called
Ways of Seeing, a series of essays on European art. For the past 20
years, however, he has lived and worked in a peasant village in the
south of France. From there he has continued to write essays on art
and on the lives of the people around him.

Like Brody, Berger recognizes that the relationship between the
peasant farmer and the animals he kills and eats is a spiritual as well as
a practical one. Again, he sees it as a relationship of interdependence
which those of us who buy our food (be it vegetable or animal) wrapped
in plastic at the supermarket cannot understand. Within our culture,
perhaps, it would be the dairy farmer who comes closest to this understanding of interdependence, this recognition that your life is dependent on the animals you care for — as their lives are dependent on you.

But back to Klass Act. In another essay, "Why Look at Animals,"
in a book called *About Looking*, Berger explores what has happened
to the city-dwellers' relationship to animals — and why shows like
Klass Act are such an apt expression of it. As we move further and
further away from a life which is directly dependent on animals
for survival, we also move further away from an understanding of

ourselves in relationship with them. Other animals become simply — animals, beings completely separate from us.

One element in this process is the romanticization of animals. Birney's bear is the forbearer, if you will, of *The Three Bears* and the Teddy Bear and even Yogi Bear. As we become more and more separate from real animals in the real world, their appearance as stuffed toys and nostalgic creatures in books and movies becomes more apparent. This becomes more marked, Berger argues, in the 19th century, as cities grow and the human species loses contact with animals. They become "things we look at," rather than beings with which we are engaged. Zoos — the London Zoo opened in 1828 — become more and more popular.

Real animals are rapidly disappearing from our lives. They have become marginalized — whether to egg and poultry farms where the hens never see the sun or to zoos or to displays like Klass Act. They are no longer at the center of our lives. As well, the people who still relate to animals in a whole way — native peoples, for example, and peasant cultures — are also marginalized. We think of them as "past" or "primitive," we display their tools in museums as artifacts, we do not think we have anything at all to learn from their way of life.

So we go to see Klass Act. We let our children be photographed with that cute tiger cub who has become as mythical a creature as Santa Claus or the Easter Bunny, whose appearances in shopping centers are also the occasion for photographs. We know nothing, anymore, about real animals.

Meanwhile, at least 20,500 dolphins are killed every year by the tuna industry, a situation allowed by the U.S. Marine Mammal Protection Act. Sometimes as many as 200 dolphins are killed for 10 tuna. They are usually bombed or netted and chopped to pieces.

Meanwhile, Beluga whales in the Gulf of St. Lawrence are producing grotesquely deformed young, if they produce at all, mainly because of the excessive industrial pollution of the Great Lakes.

Meanwhile, thousands — think of it, *thousands* — of other species become extinct or endangered every year.

When are we going to realize — or remember? We are not on the planet alone. We are in relationship with everything that lives here. And we are only one more species, after all.

■ ■ ■ ■ ■

Learning the Possibilities in Our Limitations

It was the southern fiction writer Flannery O'Connor who said "limitation and possibility mean about the same thing." It's in an essay about writing (about Catholic novelists, actually) and she says, "It is well to remember what is obvious but usually ignored: that every writer has to cope with the possibility in his given talent. Possibility and limitation mean about the same thing. It is the business of every writer to push his talent to its outermost limit, but this means the outermost limit of the kind of talent he has."

I have always liked the phrase, as I like all of O'Connor's work. And I don't think it's just about writing, either. I like what it says about paying attention to our limitations, learning to see them not as restrictions which we must strive to transcend, but as guides to the possibility of what we are. I like how it affirms the importance of paying close attention to who we are, *as we are*. And if I had to sum up my credo for living in one sentence, I think I'd choose that one.

It's a credo I think about, always, at this time of year when all of my available time is spent in my garden. Besides teaching me patience, gardening has taught me how important it is to see one's limitations as possibilities (as well, of course, as the other way around).

This is most particularly true in city gardens. And given that humans have been living in cities for several thousand years now, it's not surprising that the possibilities we have found for growing everything from cucumbers and watermelons to bonsai trees in incredibly small spaces are almost endless and always surprising. Most of them —

from the simple ones, like growing potatoes in a barrel to the most stunningly beautiful and complex Japanese gardens — have to do with *using* the limitations that small spaces impose.

Another aspect of city gardening that I really like is the fact that my garden is only part of a larger whole. On my street where there are relatively few backyard fences, this is particularly enjoyable. I like the way my wildflower garden (and somewhat haphazard, wildflower style) looks beside my neighbor's neat displays of red geraniums. I like to gaze through my bamboo cucumber teepee, over the next neighbor's magnificent poppies, through the next lady's lilies, and into the *next* yard where the beans climb the gnarled wood trellis the man there builds for them every year. Gradually our gardens intermingle too; someone is always giving a root or a cutting to someone else. The neighborhood cats are known everywhere by name, and the noises of children playing mingles pleasantly with someone else's rock music and the steady hammering of someone else working on his shed.

In my simple-minded poet's way I'd always thought that what was going on here with the vegetables and flowers and cats and neighbors was ecology, in its fullest sense. I'd even read it, right there in my *Oxford*: "ecology: that branch of biology which deals with the relations of living organisms to their surroundings, their habits and modes of life, etc."

I'd further thought, in my dreaminess, that if we managed the planet the way I manage my garden, that if we all conducted ourselves the way my neighbors and I conduct ourselves, we might be on the way to making the planet a liveable place for everyone. I wasn't saying that this was all it would take to end war and prevent famine forever, but I was sort of thinking hazily that this was the route we should take if we wanted that to happen. Paying attention, to everything, all the time. Limitation and possibility mean about the same thing. That sort of thing.

Well, I'm no scientist. So, you can be sure I was pretty awed to open up my *Globe and Mail* during a coffee break from building a stone path over by my beans on a recent Saturday morning to find out that I was off base. Completely wrong. Absolutely out there in poet's la-la-land.

To understand the ecology of this planet you have to spend $30 million dollars to build Biosphere II.

Biosphere II? $30-million? Yep. Out there in Arizona they've built this 164-metre-long fully enclosed biosphere which contains a desert, a grassy savannah, an ocean, a fresh-water marsh and a farm as well as 3,800 species of plants and animals. Make that 3,801 come 1990 when eight specially selected people will go into the biosphere and live there for two years. They're going to study ecology. One of the reasons they are going to study ecology there is to check out the possibility of such a biosphere on Mars or some other planet. This one's kinda messed up, so we'll just move on, eh?

They actually refer to this Biosphere II as an ark.

Okay, okay, I'll admit, it *is* sort of intriguing. The science-fiction fan in me sort of likes the idea of what's going to happen to those eight people, what they're going to learn about themselves and their environment over those two years. And the article does go on at great and serious length about all the experiments they're going to do and how they will help us understand things.

On the other hand, why can't they just put $30-million into paying more attention to wherever they are, when they're there, while they're there, rather than making it into someplace else? What's wrong with just taking a good, hard look at Biosphere I? While we still can.

I'm not a scientist, I'm a poet. What do I know? Well, I know this about water, for one thing. A person needs five litres of water each day for cooking and drinking. A further 25.45 litres are needed per person to stay clean and healthy. In large parts of this planet, the entire family's water is fetched daily by women and children. The most one woman can carry per trip is about 15 litres. To carry enough water for a family which included her husband, her mother and five children, a woman would have to carry 40 litres just to provide enough to drink. And 200 litres if they were to stay clean and healthy. Daily.

In many many places on this planet — most of Africa, for

instance — the source of water, a well or a standpipe, is often several kilometres away. In many places, dehydration is a major cause of sickness and death because the amount of water consumed is dependent on the amount that can be carried in a day.

Meanwhile on the same planet, here in Canada, 22 litres of water are used each time a toilet is flushed. It takes 150,000 litres to produce a ton of steel.

This, in my opinion, is ecology. We in Canada share this very small planet with several million other people. At present, our extravagance means their death. This is a limitation. We could see it as a possibility, if we chose, and therefore change what needed to be changed so that fewer people would die unnecessarily.

My objection to Biosphere II is that it assumes that the earth's limitation can be somehow *transcended*. We can use our technology to build a biosphere so we can find a solution to the "problem." We can use our technology to go to another planet, thereby leaving the "problem" behind. Somehow, the solution does not involve looking seriously at who we are, where we are, now.

We in North America assume that our culture, our way of life, our technology are the future. Yet if we look around, if we study ecology, we might notice that the starving woman in Kenya, the family in Soweto, the street child in Bogota are, by their sheer numbers, just as likely to be the future — of all of us. That's ecology, too. Maybe we should pay attention.

■ ■ ■ ■ ■

Celebrating the Cadence of a Particular Voice

One of my favorite quotes comes from the Irish poet W. B. Yeats: "The argument I have with others I call rhetoric; the argument I have with myself I call poetry." It expresses what I feel about my own writing, about the need for different kinds of "arguments" and the importance of recognizing which sort belongs where. As a poet who writes rhetorical essays, I appreciate the public voice that that craft requires, a way of articulating a clear position on events and issues. As a political person who writes poetry, I know the need for the intimate, inner argument that is the center of a poem.

Sometimes I read something by another writer, hear a speech or a poetry reading, in which both voices are present — and to which both voices in me respond. Such events send me on long journeys down paths of thought I don't usually explore. New vistas open, points of view I'd never come at quite that way before.

Listening to Angela Davis last week was one such experience for me. What follows is my response to what she said. This is not a review or a report or an analysis. Think of it as an "open letter," perhaps. Part meditation. Part rough notes for future articles and poems.

Because I am a poet I want to begin with the voice. The voice of a woman of color. I want to celebrate the particular cadence of that voice, the way it rose and fell, its almost poetic lilt, its unexpected pauses and emphases. A voice very unlike the voices I usually hear, the voices of white, male politicians, media personalities, scholars.

Each voice is both the expression of what is unique in the speaker and the evocation of what is shared with others. Sometimes we can tell a person's class background by his or her voice; we can often determine education, race, country of origin, even the region of that country. In each voice, many other voices speak. When most of the voices we hear come from one class or one gender, we lose important reminders of our diversity and our complexity as a species.

A black woman, speaking with authority, from her experience of the world. For a predominantly white audience, this is an opportunity to approach histories we have not heard, stories that have been silenced.

The story that Angela Davis tells is the story of collective action on the part of ordinary people to change their lives. Recently, this story has not been a very popular one. We like to believe it has gone "out of fashion," like Angela Davis and other prominent figures of the sixties. We prefer the story that the "sixties are over"; hippies have become yuppies and the universe of conspicuous consumption is unfolding as it should.

Such a view ignores the politics of the period in favor of an image of young, misguided people who have finally settled down to buying things. Behind that image, is the assumption that there was nothing seriously wrong anyway. It ignores the power of the civil rights movement, of the anti-war movement, of the birth and development of the present feminist movement. It ignores the reasons for those movements. It blots out the images of children in flames in Vietnam, of My Lai, of Kent State. It can forget Black Panther Fred Hampton's blood-stained bedroom after police shot him in his sleep, or the sight of Bobby Seale in chains, at the trial of the Chicago Seven, the only one in chains and the only accused who was black.

The stories we tell ourselves determine a great deal: what we understand of our past, how we view our present, what we think is possible or impossible. The extent to which we forget about Vietnam is the extent to which we will tolerate U.S. interference in Nicaragua. The extent to which we believe that racism is something that happened "back then" is the extent to which we will ignore the growing racial violence both in the U.S. and in Canada. The extent to which we ignore the power of collective actions (like the continued popular opposition to free trade in this country) is the extent of our powerlessness.

One of the things I liked about Angela Davis' speech was its passion. Ours is a culture which puts "opinion" at the bottom of our hierarchy of acceptable forms of discourse. We value facts, objectivity, statistics, as if these things were "neutral," unaffected by subjectivity. Yet even in the "hard" sciences that branch of investigation known as New Physics has begun to talk about how much of our "scientific" data is biased by assumptions about the physical world that we have not questioned. When we ask for "just the facts ma'am" we delude ourselves, just as we delude ourselves when we talk about "the truth" as if there were only one.

This does not mean that Angel Davis's talk was devoid of facts. On racism in education, for example, she noted that the number of black students enrolled in post-secondary institutions decreased (both in percentages and in actual numbers) between 1976 and 1986. In 1976 blacks represented 9.4 per cent of the college population; in 1984, 8.8 per cent. Yet more blacks than ever are prepared to enter college, a rise from 67 per cent in 1976 to 75.6 per cent in 1986. More black students drop out because of financial problems; more blacks need financial help. There are five times more black college students from families with incomes under $12,000 than white students. Such figures indicate the increasing poverty of the black population of the U.S. — and the lack of opportunity for young blacks to break out of that poverty.

One of the stories our society particularly likes to tell is the story of the individual. "Individual rights," "individual opportunity," "individualism" are some of our favorite words. Sometimes we assume that our history is only the history of great individuals, that the only important present news is news of great men and women.

The story of the individual is a great story. It celebrates all that is unique and quirky and particular and, in a sense, immortal in each of us. But it is not the only story. For many cultures, including many native cultures in this country, it is not even the most important story. If we do not hear other stories, we create a vision of society in which the needs of the whole society — or even of large groups within that society — are often seen in *opposition* to the "rights" of the individual.

Angela Davis reported that the Supreme Court recently ruled that an affirmative action program for visible minorities in Richmond, Virginia was "unconstitutional." Such a ruling threatens other such programs in 32 states. Like the opposition to such programs here, this view grows from the assumption that these programs "threaten" individual rights.

This argument ignores the fact that great individuals are as much the product of their historical and social conditions as they are of their own efforts. We could even say that the labor of thousands of working people, slaves and women over centuries has amounted to an "affirmative action program" for the "individual achievements" of rich, white men.

A woman of color speaking with feeling about the power of collective action. A vision of the world in which there is a balance between the individual and the collective, in which it is recognized that equal rights for individuals require equal possibilities — and that those *possibilities* grow from collective action. In our culture such views often get lumped in what we call the "communist camp." This is the story we tell ourselves about the world we live in.

Such a story denies the diversity of socialist experiments currently being undertaken on this planet. It denies that each has a unique history and particular characteristics. It denies what can be learned from those native cultures here which have a collective vision, even though they fly no ideological flag. By dividing the world into left and right, we divide it into "wrong" and "right." "Leftist Manley Wins in Jamaica," reads the headline of an "objective" new story. At once we are positioned in relation to what we will read. Funny. I don't recall reading "Rightist Bush Wins in the U.S.A." By dividing the world this way, we can be outraged by the activities of the U.S.S.R. in Poland, blind to the activities of U.S. multinationals in El Salvador and Chile.

A woman of color, speaking with passion, affirming collective acts of persistent men and women to overcome racism, sexism, the power of privilege, celebrating these actions as an important part of who we are. In the usual drone of political discourse in this culture, her voice was an exception. What her presence evoked, more than anything else, was the absence, in our daily lives, of voices like hers. Too bad. Now, more than ever, we need such voices.

■2■

The Family
& Other Stories

■ ■ ■ ■ ■

Domestic Violence: What Is the Connection between Home and School?

When I was asked by the organizers of these workshops to give a keynote address, I must admit that I was very nervous about accepting. I'm still very nervous about being here. My nervousness arises from the fact that I myself am not a social worker or a teacher, yet I have been asked to speak to you on issues that concern you on a daily basis. And since I'm up here talking and you're down there listening, I get to be regarded as the "expert" in these matters when in fact I am not.

My entire "social work" experience is a two-year stint as a counselor at Interval House in Kingston, Ontario, and my entire teaching experience, with the exception of creative writing workshops in public school, high schools, and university is nil. In addition, I have very little past experience of the classroom, since my own school career was spent mainly in the hall in front of the principal's office where I was sent, fairly it seems to me, for not paying attention and for talking too much.

Perhaps, though, not paying attention and talking too much have paid off. Most of my working life now, as a writer, is spent staring out the window, daydreaming, giving poetry readings and speeches like this one because I have the gift of gab. What I want to avoid today, however, is speaking to you about your jobs in that dreamy, theoretical way that keynote speakers often do and that poets almost always do. I don't want to set up a situation where I talk too much about how things should be while leaving it up to you to get out there and actually do it.

So what I'm going to talk about first of all today is what I know most about. And that is stories. All my life I have been listening to stories, reading stories, finding ways of using stories in my poetry and nowadays writing them myself. What I want to talk about first of all today, then, is what we might call the Stories of Our Culture, the Stories we all participate in and believe to be about "Us."

For those of you who are wondering how all this relates to the question of the connection between domestic violence in the home and what goes on in school, I'd say "a lot" and promise you that in my sneaky writer's way, by indirection, I will get to it. As a hint, I'll add that I think some of the "answer" to that question lies in the fact that we have to ask it at all. The question, in fact, implies that "home" is one place and "school" is another and what goes on in one may or may not be connected to what happens in the other. This idea of private spheres, in fact, is one of the strongest myths of our culture, one of our most popular stories if you will. And nowhere is it stronger than in what I call The Story of The Family.

The Story of The Family is most certainly our strongest, most powerful story. Everyone tells it. Everyone talks about The Family. Everyone evokes it as what must be protected against the evil of the moment: drugs, or abortion, or aids, or communism, or street violence, or whatever.

Of course, everyone also lives in a family. Strangely enough, however, living in the family is, if you will, often a very different story from the actual Story of The Family. And that's part of the problem. But I'm getting ahead of myself. First of all I have to tell you the Story of The Family.

Now, to tell you this story, I could have chosen the Bible, or any of a million novels. I could have chosen a song or a movie. I could even have chosen a McDonald's commercial because, as I've said, the story of the family is everywhere. And we're all shaped by it. Although we all have our own personal experience of the family, we very often measure that experience, judge that experience if you will, by The Story of The Family that is being told by the culture at large. So the version of the story that I have chosen is the one that I think is probably familiar to a great many of you and that, if TV ratings are any indication (and I think they are), is a very important story for a very great many people.

I'm talking about the "Bill Cosby Show." If there is a perfect example of the modern version of The Story of The Family, this is surely it.

Now, there are a number of things that I like about this story. For one thing, I recognize it as another version of The Story of The Family that I grew up with which was "Father Knows Best." In *that* version, of course, you had Margaret and Jim Anderson and their three kids, Betty, Bud, and Kathy. Jim worked at some job that required him to wear a suit and tie and carry a briefcase, and Margaret was a housewife.

As the Story of The Family for the 1980s, Bill Cosby's Huxtable family are a little different from the Andersons, of course. They're black, for one thing. And Claire Huxtable works outside the home as a lawyer. Cliff Huxtable (Cosby) is a doctor, an obstetrician as a matter of fact. There are also five children in this family.

However, in many ways, the story hasn't changed a bit. I want to outline briefly some of the themes of The Story of The Family which the "Bill Cosby Show" works on in telling its particular version.

Problems faced by family members often come from outside the family: peer pressure, school, work, etc. These problems and those within the family are always resolved within the family and always by discussion. The Huxtables are presented as reasonable, caring parents who are able to help their children in every imaginable predicament and the Huxtables' children usually take the advice their parents offer. In almost every situation, the parents' advice is "good" advice and everything always works out okay. What is presented is The Story of The Family in which affection and openness, both between the adults and between adults and children is natural and easy. It is also present-ed as natural and easy for the children to "look up to" and turn to their parents for advice.

Now, let's look a little deeper at this Story and what it tells us. First of all, let's look at the fact that the family is organized in what I call a Benevolent Hierarchy. Dad, Mom, children (in descending order of age). Dad, though he is sometimes portrayed as having quirks or exhibiting foolishness, is generally an Excellent Parent. In other words, his authority as the head of the family is not seriously challenged, is seen, in fact, as natural and good. This is further reinforced, incidently, by the fact that Bill Cosby himself writes books on parenting.

Mom is next in the hierarchy and "The Bill Cosby Show" works hard at being relatively non-sexist. Still, much of the show's humor derives from stereotypical incidents of "female irrationality" (her fear of mice, for example, or from incidents where Cliff or one of the kids has to try some subtle subterfuge to "get around" her). Still, she is a "good mother" despite the fact that she has a high-powered demanding job. In fact, it's sometimes hard to believe that either of the Huxtables works outside the home since they are almost always there, always relaxed, and always ready to have a long heart-to-heart.

The idea of Benevolent Hierarchy functions equally well among the children. The older children are portrayed as being caring and concerned for their younger siblings. The one boy is "kept in line" by his sisters. None of these kids ever fights for very long. They respect their parents, they seek their support and advice. They take that advice. This is all presented as natural, easy and "the way things should be."

What "The Cosby Show" presents as The Story of The Family, of course, is a story that we all want very much to believe. That's one of the reasons why it is so very popular. It presents a view of the family that our society cherishes and believes to be the way the family "really is."

Or rather, the way the family "really could be" if only all these bad things weren't destroying it. And by "all these bad things" I mean, of course, all the things I mentioned before — and any others that we care to mention (feminism, sex education in the schools). "All these bad things" which, like the writers of "The Cosby Show," we like to see as attacking the family from the *outside*, to change it from what it "really is."

The way the family "really is." Let's think about that for a moment. Let's think about it in the context of why we are all here today.

We are here today because in our everyday, working lives, as teachers and social workers and yes, even as writers, we are confronted with family situations which are very different from the one seen on "The Bill Cosby Show." We are here because in a very large number of families in this society (2 in 10) women are beaten regularly by their partners, children are the observers of that violence, and are the victims of parental violence themselves.

We are here, too, because we want to do something to change this situation and because we need to know how. And in order to learn how, we have to think about why. And to help in thinking about why, the organizers of the conference have asked people like me to come and talk. And so far, I've talked about "The Bill Cosby Show." What's the connection?

As I said before, one of the elements in The Story of The Family is that it's always being attacked from the outside. And very often, in discussions of domestic violence against women and children, there is a tendency to look for the causes of that violence in the same way. Men are violent, this story goes, because of job pressures, or financial pressures, because they drink too much, or abuse drugs, or feel threatened by the ways in which feminism is changing women's role.

This is a comforting story because it means that the family is really okay except in a few cases. In other words, domestic violence is someone else's story, not ours.

The problem I have with these explanations as "reasons" for domestic violence is that they raise more questions than they answer. They don't explain, for example, why all these pressures lead men to act violently only in relation to their wives or why, in fact, violence is a logical reaction to these problems in the first place. They don't explain why violence against women and children has a history as long as the history of the family itself, or why a man's right to beat his wife was until recently enshrined in law.

For me, these "explanations" are a way of avoiding the need to look at *the family itself*, at its structure, at our assumptions about it, at the expectations we have of it, as the source of domestic violence against women and children.

What happens if we look at the structure of the family itself and its connection to domestic violence? For me, this means looking at the hierarchy of the family, that hierarchy which seems so benevolent and workable in something like "The Cosby Show," and asking why? Why do we assume that it's "natural" or "good" that the family should be structured with the father as the "head," assuming all the power for leadership and control which that metaphor implies? Why do we assume that father always "knows best" in relation to the rest of the family or even that parents always "know best" in relation to their children?

We have to ask these questions, I think, because in a great many cases, this structure that we think of as natural and benevolent doesn't work. It doesn't work because it is based on the idea that having control over others by virtue of gender or age, and enforcing that control by whatever means necessary, is also natural and benevolent. All in the Family, if you will.

Study after study of men who batter their wives indicates that these men generally have very traditional ideas of men's and women's roles in society and in the family, that they feel they should have absolute control over the family situation and that their violence, in fact, grows out of their inability to maintain that control at all times. In the same way, much of the violence that parents commit against their children comes out of notions of discipline that stem from the belief that they must be in total control, or out of frustration at not being able to maintain that control.

What we need to ask, as social workers or teachers or writers or human beings, I think, is who says? Who says that men and women and children have to be a certain way in the family by virtue of sex, or age any more than they do by virtue of the length of their noses, or the shape of their ears? And who says that this sort of family, this traditional mommy / daddy / kids, is the only "real family," or even the one we should all try to emulate?

The first "connection," it seems to me, is in the need to question these assumptions wherever possible. One of the best places to question, it seems to me, would be in the educational system. What better place than a classroom to get people thinking about the nature of the family, about all the different kinds of families, and about how those families work. In any given classroom there are likely to be children from traditional families, extended families, single parent (of either sex) families, families where one parent is now in a homosexual relationship, perhaps. All sorts of possibilities that could be explored as a way of talking about and looking critically at our assumption that there is only one "real family."

Another story that I want to mention briefly at this point is the story of violence itself — or rather, what our culture seems to consider to be justified violence. Again I want to look at TV for a minute. You've all, I'm sure, heard some sort of horrifying statistic about the number of violent incidents that the average child will see on TV before he or she turns 18. Somewhere, I believe, between 10 and 50 thousand. Very often, these statistics are brought out in discussions about the effect of TV violence on children. This has the effect, again, like some of the discussions about the "causes" of domestic violence, of putting the problem out there, laying the blame somewhere else.

Another way to look at it is to see the incidence of TV violence as an *expression* of a culture which increasingly accepts violence in one form or another as an acceptable means of resolving conflict. It's harder to look at it this way, of course, because "a culture" means us. Means everyone here in this room. Means how you honked at the person in front of you this morning when they didn't move as soon as the light turned green. Or how you say to your kid, without thinking about it, maybe even "jokingly": "If you don't cut that out, I'll kill you, I mean it."

I'm sure you can all come up with your own personal examples. They may not be *physically* violent, obviously, but they involve threats, threatening gestures, raised voices, threatening expressions as an acceptable means of getting someone else to do what you want them to do. And that, for me, is a continuum which runs through the man who beats his wife, to the convenience store owner who shoots someone who robs him, to the fighting that breaks out on the average picket line, to the troops whose presence is accepted in Dublin or Beirut or the small villages of Nicaragua, to the fact that all our lives are hostage to the idea that the differences between the super-powers could be adequately resolved by the presence of nuclear weapons.

It seems to me that we have come to the point, almost, where the concept of resolving conflict *any other way* is unthinkable. That's why, perhaps, the hierarchical structures that operate in almost every aspect of social groupings — from the family to the military — seem "natural." Are they really natural or are we no longer able to explore the possibility of alternatives?

I want to explain what I mean more concretely by looking for a minute at the school system, at the hierarchies that exist there, and at the effect of our assumptions that these hierarchies are "natural."

Most obvious, of course, is the structure of the average classroom itself, with its one teacher and 25-30 odd students. There are lots of questions we could ask here about why we assume that one man or woman is capable of meeting the needs of that many students, and I'm sure teachers present could talk about the problems that arise because such a situation is often humanly impossible. And of course we all know that student reactions to these situations — discipline problems as they are often called, or laziness, or not working to potential, or disruptiveness — are regarded as *the problem* and not the situation that creates them. There's a parallel here, of course, with some of the thinking that somehow domestic violence is "caused" because the *victims* act or don't act in a particular way.

I want to say at this point, that as a parent my experience of most teachers is that they are well aware of the problems created by the traditional classroom structure and are often frustrated by it. I also know there are lots of unemployed teachers around *and* lots of situations — if my son's experience is any indication — where children enjoy the opportunity to learn from and teach each other. I think the question we have to ask ourselves as a society is why we accept an educational system that teaches children from a very early age to accept a hierarchical structure with all the emphasis on control and respect for "authority" that that implies.

I also want to raise some other questions about the nature of schools and the hierarchies that exist there, but I want to emphasize first that I'm not saying that the schools *invent* these hierarchies. I believe that students enter the schools with a basic acceptance of hierarchy as a "natural" structure of society already in place. What I'm questioning is why the schools, of all places, never challenge that acceptance.

A whole lecture, for example, could be spent on the class bias that exists in the structure of our high schools. As you know, students are early on divided into Advanced, General or Basic Level courses of study, with the Advanced being charted for university, while the General and the Basic are directed more towards community colleges or technical training. I don't think it's accidental that there is a very definite relationship between the students in each particular course of study and their class background. Not surprisingly, there are more professors' children in the Advanced level courses, more factory workers' kids in the General. Is this because working-class children are not as bright as middle-class kids? Or because there is a predisposition within the school system to accept certain class biases as "natural" or "inevitable." It's like the old observation that IQ tests don't measure intelligence as much as they measure the student's parent's economic status. It's interesting, in this regard, that a recent survey of local students done by the *Whig-Standard* indicated that most students were going to university. But on close reading, that became most students who were in Grades 12 or 13. This means, mostly students in the Advanced level courses. Middle-class kids.

Another story then. This one's about how most kids go to college. But what about all the kids in the General and Basic level courses that *didn't* get interviewed by the *Whig*. What do they want, expect, hope for the future. What would their stories be?

If the schools accept a class hierarchy, they also accept a gender hierarchy. Not too long ago *The Globe and Mail* published a story about a report recently released by a committee set up to study Government-approved reading materials in Ontario schools. Some interesting facts:

– the world presented in these textbooks is one in which boys are "vastly over-represented." For example, boys handled equipment, played piano, danced, argued, collected stickers and protected mussels. Girls became afflicted with "the vanity of city girls," abandoned a ballet recital, went on a diet, dreamed sad dreams, and cried.

– women performed 15 tasks compared with men who took on 45 different activities. Women's tasks included being a loyal friend, eyeing a letter suspiciously, bossing neighbours, and being sick with a headache. Men's tasks included investigating a kidnapping, acting in silent films, operating a restaurant chain.

– most female adventures involved watching others have adventures, being captured and not surviving.

I could go on, but I think you get the point. These facts are based on studies of texts read by children in grade 4, 5, and 6.

High school is, if anything, worse. I've already mentioned the class bias. In a study done by Susan Russell, a sociology professor at Concordia University (*The Hidden Curriculum of School*), some interesting facts, based on observations of 27 grade 12 classes come to light:

– girls were found to dominate in verbal interaction with the teacher in only 7 per cent of the exchanges, boys in 63 per cent, minor discrepancies by sex in the remainder.

– teachers directed between one and a half and five times as many questions to boys as to girls. (English / Chemistry).

– in all classes boys asked more questions, made more comments.

– several comments by teachers indicated that they preferred boys' classroom behavior: boys were perceived as being "pointed in their questions," girls as "vague"; boys "don't hold grudges," girls take themselves too seriously; boys were seen more as "open," girls less forthright.

– regarding high achievers: "boys have got there completely on their cleverness, but the girls who are there tend to be the ones who have worked."

– girls who declined in their achievement were seen as working according to their ability; boys who declined were seen as under-achieving.

I could go on with more examples, but my point here — and in the study itself — is that these ways of looking at boys and girls were not questioned by the teachers, were accepted, in fact, as "natural," and the way boys and girls "were."

What all this means to me is that as a culture we have come to accept a very limited view of what it means to be a human being. We accept that men can and should do certain things and that women can and should do certain other things. We accept that the family should be a certain way and should perform certain functions in society. When there are problems, we assume that people aren't doing what they "should," rather than that there's something wrong with the expectations we have for them.

I think that the root cause of family violence lies in our accep-tance of this limited view of men and women and of the family; in our acceptance of social structures in which one person or group of persons has power over another group by virtue of gender, age, class, whatever; in our acceptance that conflict between individuals or between groups can be resolved by enforcing that power, with violence if necessary. These are the dominant stories of our culture. To the extent that we all continue to tell these stories and these stories only, without exam-ining them critically, we participate in the situation we are here today to resolve.

The story of domestic violence against women and children is a story about us, about everyone in this room. It is also a story we can change. I think that it's important to remember that because these structures — these ways of looking at each other, at the family, at the world — are culturally invented, rather than natural, means that we can change them. And I'd like to end on an optimistic note by outlining what that change would mean in a concrete, personal way.

I am the mother of a 13-year-old son. Like all parents in this culture, I am only one influence on him, on his attitudes and opinions, on how he will be in the world. I am a major influence, certainly, but only one and, as he grows older, a less dominant one. As a member of a society I rely on other citizens to help in the process of preparing my son for his adult world. I am supposed to trust them. I need them to reinforce and enlarge upon the things I try to teach him. Here are some of the things I hope he learns.

I'll start with school. In history class, I hope he learns that besides the stories of what men have done in the past, which fill the history books, there are also stories of women's deeds which are not present. I want him to learn to ask why? In English class, I want him to learn to ask again where women's stories are, and why we have a language in which the male gender is used to speak for the whole species and what that means about how we look at the world. In health class I hope he will learn to talk openly about his body, about his feelings, about sexual relations, and about his needs, fears, hopes, and responsibilities in these relations, regardless of whether he chooses to have those relationships with women or with men. In social science, I hope he will be taught to look critically at the society in which he lives, and to question whether its organization — from the family unit to the government — is the "way it has to be" or the way we've chosen it to be for now and why? In gym class, I hope he learns to dance as well as to play basketball, and I hope he learns to play basketball to have fun, not just to win.

I could go on, but you get my point. It scares me to think that my son is learning to be "a man" in this culture, because when I look around and see what a man is, I don't like what I see. In this culture men may make more money and have better jobs than women do, but they are also responsible for the fact that most women can expect to be beaten or raped some time in their lives and that a girl child has more chance of being sexually assaulted than she does of needing glasses. I don't want to believe that this happens because men are naturally more aggressive or violent than women any more than they are naturally smarter or more organized or better able to drive trucks.

In fact, I think that's nonsense. I also think that there's a connection, a big connection, between the fact that we assume men are better able to drive trucks or boss other people around and the fact that they are responsible for beating and raping women and children. That's the connection I see between education and domestic violence: the connection between how we are taught to see ourselves and what we are capable of doing. Right now that connection limits and hurts everyone. I don't think it has to. I think it can free and heal us too.

■ ■ ■ ■ ■

Feminists, Like Explorers, Spend Their Lives Venturing into Unknown Territory

Not long ago, someone asked me how I became a feminist. We had just met and were having our first conversation during a coffee break, in the middle of a busy day. I tried to answer her, but 15 minutes just wasn't enough.

"Think about it," my new friend said, as she got up to rinse her cup, "maybe you could write me a letter sometime."

She was half-joking, but now that I have thought about it, a letter seems a very good idea:

Dear Susan,

You asked how I "*became* a feminist" and when you put it like that, it sounds a little as if you think it happened with a blinding flash of light, like Saul on the road to Damascus, changing me completely, all at once. I have been changed, definitely, but it's a much slower process. I haven't so much become a feminist as I am *becoming* one.

In that sense, I am like the people I know who are sincere pacifists, or truly religious. What we share, it seems to me, is the recognition that strong convictions are a lot like maps. They guide us through the world, certainly, but they have to be checked, constantly, for accuracy. There's a lot of unknown territory out there; new routes have to be charted, whole countries named.

Feminism, especially, involves a journey into unknown territory. It is a journey into places where women have been absent, the blank spaces in history, psychology, science, literature, art, music, religion, anthropology, and politics where women's lives have not been adequately recorded.

My journey began 20 years ago this month. A group called the Student Union for Peace Action, one of the forerunners of current peace groups, was meeting at Queen's. This was during the 1960s, when lots of people my age were talking about "changing the system" and "building a new world," though what went on, really, was that the men did most of the talking; the women listened. Some of us tried to speak once in a while, but no one paid much attention.

This time, however, the women decided to meet separately for a while. I remember wondering, as we left the room, what we were going to talk about. I couldn't imagine.

What we talked about was how we had joined the peace group because we saw things around us that we wanted to change, but what we found was that we were still held back by the one thing no one even talked of changing: the relationship between men and women. I didn't know then that a lot of people (from Pearl S. Buck to Karl Marx) have noted that understanding this relationship is basic to understanding any culture, but that's what we began to explore that day.

We started with questions. Some of them we had words for; some were just "in the air" as difficult questions are when they are being asked for the first time. Looking back, I'd say that many of those questions came down to one: Why does no one listen to us?

It is that question, more than anything else, that made me start to become a feminist. Trying to answer it has kept me one.

It has taken many forms. When I was still a student in English, it was: Why are there so few women writers on my courses?

When I started working it was: Why am I paid less than the man beside me, doing the same job? Why is it assumed that I won't be working very long because I'll want to stay home and raise a family? Why does it have to be either/or?

In 1973, when I was pregnant with my son, I got involved with a childbirth education group, learning the Lamaze method. But why was it so difficult to persuade doctors to support this method? Why were pregnancy and childbirth treated almost like medical emergencies, instead of natural processes? And why were so many hospital practices — enemas, shaving, routine use of anaesthetics, stirrups — seemingly designed to frustrate and complicate the natural process, while making it "easier" for the doctor? Since then, many things have changed, but new questions could be raised around the medical profession's reluctance to recognize midwives.

My son's presence in my life created a whole range of emotions. Overpowering love, yes, but also fear, anger, helplessness, impatience. I looked in vain for books that talked about these things. Why was there such silence about these ambivalent feelings? Was I the only woman who felt them?

In the last 10 years, I've worked mostly as a poet, publishing several books. But why are there so few women poets before this century? Why are there almost no women writers who wrote and raised families as well? Why do women writers, and women writers only, have to choose? This means I have very few models to learn from. There are no maps here; each poem is an entrance into an uncharted territory. For you, as a reader, it means lots of poems and stories about battles, but very few about raising children. Half of the story of what we are, as a species, is missing.

I also worked for a while as a counselor at Kingston Interval House. Why has it taken us until this decade to acknowledge that wife-battering exists, on a large scale, let alone recognize that it's a crime? Why this silence about incest, too, and child assault? Why do we go on talking about "the family" as if it always fit our happiest visions and was not, often, the source of violence, fear, and pain?

For each of us, male or female, asking such questions opens new perspectives. In that sense, feminism is a relocation; you take up a new place in the world. Like your question to me, Susan.

Now how do you respond to my answer?

■ ■ ■ ■ ■

Women's Week 'With Courage and Vision'

"Anybody may blame me who likes, when I add further . . . that then I longed for a power of vision which might overpass that limit; which might reach the busy world, towns, regions full of life I had heard of but never seen; that then I desired more of practical experience than I possessed; more of intercourse with my kind, of acquaintance with variety of character, than was here within my reach."

These words are Jane Eyre's, the heroine in Charlotte Brontë's novel by the same name. A young governess 150 years ago longs for a life beyond the confining limitations which her class and her sex have imposed upon her. She has a vision and she expects to be blamed for expressing that vision.

It is the longing — and this fear of blame — that speaks to us still. Jane's words echo in the slogan for this year's International Women's Week Celebrations in Kingston: With Courage and Vision.

Vision to imagine another sort of world. And courage, courage to make this vision happen, no matter what.

"Could you imagine a world of women only?" the interviewer asked. "Can you imagine a world where women are absent." (He believed he was joking.) Yet I have to imagine at one and the same moment, both. Because I live in both.

These words are by poet Adrienne Rich. *A world of women only*. Once a year we come together to celebrate ourselves as women. At International Women's Day events, I often see women I haven't seen all year; I get to catch up on the news. Gossip, I suppose, that word used so often to denigrate women's conversation. I prefer to see it as the oral tradition by which women explore our collective lives. I like to think that it was gossip — those few precious minutes in the kitchen, while the men talked politics in the front room — that kept my foremothers strong and sane. Like any oral tradition, gossip is necessary when you can't read about yourself in the books your society produces.

And there's lots that goes on besides gossip. There are seminars and lectures and workshops. Respectable gossip, I guess. Ways we have found to speak into the silences that history has left in women's lives.

Can you imagine a world where women are absent? Of course. I live in one. If I look in the history books, I seldom find myself and when I do, I am always the exception — Joan of Arc, Elizabeth I, Abbess Hildegard. Sometimes my presence in history is a shameful embarrassment, as in the case of Pope Joan. But more often, I am simply *not there*; it is as if what I did all day, what I thought, how I lived, how I spoke were irrelevant to the life of the species, impossible to imagine or too insignificant to record.

And today? Well, I go to the movies and watch women being frightened and raped and beaten. I see our naked bodies displayed in everything from *Playboy* to an ad for some soft drink. Everywhere I look I see myself through the eyes of men. But I am always silent. The rape victim's story, the prostitute's, the cover-girl's. Where are they? What are we so afraid of hearing that we never let them speak for themselves?

I turn on the TV and watch "The Cosby Show" or "Family Ties."

I let myself believe that the "real family" is like that. Certainly, there is no evidence to the contrary. The battered wife does not get to tell her story. Nor does the incest victim. The single mother on welfare is not heard from. Nor do we want to listen to the lesbian mother whose children have been taken from her because she does not fit our notion of a "normal mom."

Silence from the increasing number of families who are homeless in North America, from the 12,000 children (average age: 5) who are homeless in New York City alone. Silence from the thousands of families in Canada who are destroyed daily by poverty, unemployment, or the long-term effects of shift-work. Silence from the immigrant families threatened by this country's racism, from the refugee families who aren't even allowed to enter because we have "no room." Not a word from the native women who watch their children destroy themselves with drugs and alcohol, their culture ruined because it doesn't fit the white norm.

A silence that is imposed, not chosen. In fact, the story of the Keatons' family, or the Cosbys', is the story of the minority. Yet it is their story alone that gets told. Whose interests does its telling serve? And why?

International Women's Day grew from the struggle of women garment workers to form a union in the United States at the turn of the century. On March 8, 1907, a demonstration took place in which women demanded decent wages and the 10-hour day.

Today we're still demanding decent wages, wages equal to those of men performing similar tasks. Why is it so difficult? Why is the answer so often "Wait. What you ask is expensive. It will have a negative effect on business."

As I see it, employers have made huge profits by paying women less than men. For years now. In a very real sense, they owe us millions. The demand for equal pay is simply the demand that they pay up. Now.

As for the 10-hour day, well! Any woman with small children, whether she works at home or for wages, would love that. Even more, to be:

A free woman. At last free!
Free from slavery in the kitchen
where I walked back and forth stained
and squalid among cooking pots.

The words of some bitchy, modern feminist? Not on your life. that's an Indian poet (known as the Mother of Sumanjala) writing somewhere between the third and the first century B.C.

Such freedom for women can only come when the work of our species is truly shared. And again, it is within the family that this lack of sharing is most evident. Until men are willing to share the tasks that constitute the daily life of the species — cooking, cleaning, and most importantly, raising children — this lament, from a Chinese poet, Chuo Wenchun (179-177 B.C.), will still speak to many women:

Why should marriage bring only tears?
All I wanted was a man
With a single heart . . .
Not somebody always after wriggling fish
With his big bamboo rod.

Not only in the home, but in the society as a whole. Until we recognize our responsibility to children as a collective responsibility, the work of the species is not shared. Without this vision of shared work, issues such as reproductive choice and day care (and the larger health care and social welfare questions which surround them) remain "women's issues." Which is to say, issues of second-class, marginal importance, which need not be considered when we look at free trade or defence spending.

It is Adrienne Rich who says somewhere that the species progresses because of the "persistent, small act." I believe this. I believe we progress as a species because of the small acts of people who don't make it to the history books.

The woman who joins a union. The incest survivor who speaks up, and when no one listens, speaks up again. The lesbian who comes out (as so many courageous women in Kingston have, during the discussion around the human sexuality report). The man who stays home with his children while his wife works. The women who stay home now, unnoticed, because what they are doing is not "exceptional." Parents who teach their daughters how to change a tire and their sons how to cook. The teacher who uses a textbook in which girls are prominent. The little girl who asks why? Why not? And keeps on asking.

With courage and vision. The persistent small acts that together change history. The single voices that together become loud enough to fill up the silences where women have been absent.

What do women want? Everything, of course. Because anything is possible. Though "anybody may blame me who likes," I believe that.

Happy International Women's Day, sisters. Keep on keeping on.

■ ■ ■ ■ ■

Double Edged Fun

Some time ago, a friend gave me a newspaper clipping about this real fun nightclub in Toronto where the major entertainment was a gold-fish-swallowing contest. The object was to see how many a person could swallow in 30 seconds. Live, of course. And the article specifically called the place where this happened a *nightclub*. Not some crummy bar you understand, but a *nightclub*. And these were adults, too. Serious adults, *older people*, accountants and junior lawyers, probably, or engineers, the sort of people who design bridges and nuclear power plants. Drinking beer and swallowing goldfish.

Actually, the article wasn't about the goldfish-swallowing contests at all. It was about how the owner of the nightclub canceled the gold-fish-swallowing contests because of "public pressure." Isn't that nice? He didn't even *have* to either, because laws against cruelty to animals don't protect fish. Nevertheless, the Ontario Humane Society does try to persuade nightclub owners that there is a better way to make money than swallowing goldfish. No kidding!

And guess what that better way is?

Instead of "exploiting fish for the purpose of creating business," says the Humane Society inspector, "why not get into a wet T-shirt contest or mud wrestling . . . . "

Just a minute, did an adult speak to me? Yep, and he said, "why not get into a wet T-shirt contest or mud wrestling . . . . "

This is the real reason my friend gave me the article.

You'll notice that our Humane Society inspector, who is pledged to protecting exploited goldfish everywhere, doesn't even mention who's going to be wearing the T-shirts or doing the mud wrestling. But can anybody out there hazard a guess?

C'mon, now, it's not that hard. Who earns less money than a man and has less protection against exploitation than a goldfish?

You got it. The girl in the wet T-shirt.

And if you thought *that* was entertaining, you oughta love this piece, also sent to me by a reader, from another Toronto newspaper. It's about what's referred to as an "upscale strip club" in Dearborn, Michigan, where they have a wet T-shirt contest with a twist. In this one, the men in the club are given pretend Uzi submachine guns filled with water to shoot at the dancers.

Yes, you read it right. The men shoot water guns at the dancers. For fun.

As one customer says, "The excitement is turning on these women. The excitement is when you shoot." The owner of the club sees this form of entertainment as a chance for his customers to relax. "I get lots of executives in this club . . . they've got high-pressure jobs. One night a week, I give them a squirt gun and a chance to act like a little kid and loosen up a bit."

He doesn't think his "entertainment" has anything to do with hostility towards women. "I don't think these guys are hostile to women. Look at the expressions on their faces. They're smiling. It's all a game and women are part of the game — they're the object that's up there."

The object that's up there.

What is being said here? What is this man admitting about his attitude toward women without even meaning to?

Of course, these two examples of what our culture considers entertainment are not unique. Wet T-shirt contests and strip joints are pretty common, as are movies where women are made to look stupid (this is called "family entertainment") and rock videos where we are often caged or on leashes. What is particularly painful in these two cases, for me, is the level of denial among the participants. The Humane Society inspector does not name *who* will perform in the alternate entertainment he suggests. The participants in the shooting game simply see the women as objects.

Even the dancers seem to participate in this denial. One of them is quoted as saying, "Sometimes, this stuff can really depress you. It's an ego trip for these guys . . . a Rambo scene. But it's a game. I can't imagine I don't have fun."

I can't imagine I don't have fun.

Why can't she imagine that?

Having fun. It's interesting to look at the ways in which our culture has fun. To consider the number of sports in which some form of rough body contact is a necessary part of the game. To think about how much of our humor relies on put-downs, on racist or sexist stereotyping (Newfie jokes, Jewish mother jokes, mother-in-law jokes). To try and count the number of movies in which the central action is a woman being humiliated or frightened or hurt. What do our ways of playing say about us?

Perhaps the owner of the "upscale strip club" should have the last word on entertainment. Perhaps he knows his culture better than the "experts" who think the game he permits in this bar is dangerous.

"Psychologists don't know why guys do it," he says. "It's like playing splatball (shooting paint pellets from a gun) with some of the guys on the weekend. It's the same thing."

Shooting women for fun. Shooting the other guys for fun. Great fun. They say it beats swallowing goldfish.

■ ■ ■ ■ ■

And What Are Little Girls Made of . . . ?

There's a poem by Canadian poet P. K. Page that's always been one of my favorites. It's called "Little Girls" and it begins:

More than discovery — rediscovery.
They renew
acquaintanceship with all things
as with flowers in dreams.

And delicate as a sketch made by being
they merge in a singular way with
their own thoughts . . .

She has another, too, called "Young Girls" which has the wonderful opening line: "Nothing, not even fear of punishment / can stop the giggle in a girl."

I like these poems. I like their energy and their promise and their wit. I like what they say about girls. It confirms that I like what I see in my own friends and in the girls I meet when I conduct poetry workshops in elementary and high schools. Girls who are silly and funny and brave, who write crazy, beautiful poems and stories, who want to be marine biologists and brain surgeons and truck drivers. Or clowns.

"What do you want to be when you grow up?" my friend asks her three-year-old daughter, Anna.

"A clown."

"What if you couldn't be a clown, what would you want to be?"

"An adult."

Ah, I like that. I like Anna's slightly skewed, but very wise view of her future. Better a clown than an adult any day. Especially a boring one.

All of this makes me a little sad, wishing I'd had a daughter as well as a son.

But there's another kind of sadness, too, that comes with thinking about daughters, about little girls. Both of Page's poems have a note of sadness in them. In one, she speaks of young girls being "caught and swung on the bright hooks of their sex." In the other she writes:

> Older, they become round and hard, demand
> shapes that are real, castles on the shore
> and all the lines and angles of tradition
> are mustered for them in their eagerness
> to become whole, fit themselves to the thing
> they see outside them,
> while the thing they left
> lies like a caul in some abandoned place,
> unremembered by fingers or the incredibly bright
> stones, which for a time replace their eyes.

"To . . . fit themselves to the thing they see outside them." There's a sadness in that, in the reality of most girls' futures, in the few who will make it as marine biologists or brain surgeons or truck drivers compared with the many who long to. It made me wonder what it was like to raise a daughter these days, to share both those wonderful possibilities — and the stubborn realities. I asked some of my friends, all of them strong feminists, what it was like.

"I marvel at her ability to have strong opinions about things," the mother of a three-year-old writes, "and her assertiveness. There are moments when I think it would be a lot easier if I had a more complacent, passive little girl (you know, what little girls are supposed to be like) but these moments are fleeting."

And the mother of a teenager says, "Raising a daughter is fraught with joy and anxiety that is for me different from the delights and problems of raising a son . . . the feeling of déja vu is so much stronger."

"I'm hoping my own memories will help me be understanding and sensitive to all she is going through," writes someone whose daughter is eight. "It sure sounds like the job description will increase with experience."

All three worried for their daughters a great deal. "Sometimes I think of *The Handmaid's Tale*," wrote one, referring to Margaret Atwood's bleak futurist novel where women are slaves, "and wonder if this is the world my daughter will be part of."

"My worst fears would be the wasting of her abilities," writes another, "a youthful and inappropriate relationship with unplanned children and an inability to become economically independent or to provide for her later years, since old age and poverty are often synonymous for women in our society."

Their hopes for their daughters? Independence was first on everyone's list. Integrity, self-esteem, gentleness, "a strong sense of social justice." Everyone recognized the opportunities that the feminist movement had created for them and for their daughters and all hoped that their daughters would never be "complacent about the world," but see themselves as "part of a larger community."

Statistics indicate that many of their hopes will not be realized, except, certainly, the part about not being complacent in the world. I see it in girls' faces, sometimes, when I visit the high schools, especially the senior grades. It's as if they are catching on, slowly.

"The young women are the worst off," another poet, Roo Borson, writes in a poem called "Talk":"No one has bothered to show them things. / You can see their minds on their faces, / they are like little lakes before a storm."

"I would like to be a lawyer, a psychiatrist or a dancer," writes Lynlee, age eight.

"I like being a woman," says Anna, age three.

"I hope she still says that as an adult," her mother says.

So do I, even if she decides not to be a clown.

■ ■ ■ ■ ■

Sugar Plums and Calabashes

In that famous poem about the night before Christmas, "the children are nestled all snug in their beds, while visions of sugar plums danced in their heads." Sugar plums are dancing in my head too, as Christmas approaches. They're dancing in a lot of women's heads, I'll bet. Well, not sugar plums exactly, but chocolates, certainly, especially the ones that still have to be purchased for dear Aunt Lillian. And the turkey of course. There it is waltzing away with the mince pie and the fruitcake. And then there's the glazed yams, and the stuffing, and the mashed potatoes, and the gravy, and the shortbread, and the jellied salads and . . .

All of which would be very enjoyable except that someone has to plan for all this stuff, the sugar plum fairy being stubbornly absent from most women's kitchens. Someone has to buy it and organize it and cook it. In most cases that someone will be female.

Now, I'm not saying that's all bad. I like to cook and I like to use recipes that have been handed down to me from my foremothers. I like the particularly female sense of community that comes from sharing recipes and cooking secrets. Mind you, I think it's pretty weird that our society is so organized that women do the majority of the food purchase and preparation. In most other animal species, not being able to feed yourself makes you a candidate for extinction, but then we humans have managed to set things up in such a way that even the most bizarre practices seem normal.

Women and food is one of them. And because our need for food is so basic, women's almost exclusive relationship to it has fundamental and far-reaching consequences. Women are so deeply connected with our ideas of nurturing that it appears to be simply "natural," so that men's absence from that aspect of our lives seems natural too.

Yet, like any other human activity, our practices around food are socially created. And like any other socially created practice, they are gendered. As a result, our relationship to food is complex, often contradictory and frequently dangerous.

Take women and fat, for example. Strange, isn't it, that in a society in which women are expected to be good cooks and are valued for their nurturing qualities, we are also expected to be boyishly thin. Women who obviously nurture *themselves* and who, as a result, are somewhat plump, are considered socially unattractive. A recent ad for weight-loss products said it all. It pictured a young, pretty, plump woman with the caption, "I was tired of being told I had a nice personality." Very economical, that. How it manages to insult woman's mind *and* her body in one sentence.

Taken further, this contradiction results in several deaths each year, especially among young women. Anorexia nervosa is a condition in which women (and some young men) literally starve themselves to conform to an over-exacting idea of perfect thinness. Thousands of others suffer from other forms of eating disorders which severely affect their health. The causes of these disorders are complex, but one factor is certainly a neurotic concern with body-image (and the fear of being fat) which is socially conditioned.

Indeed, the focus on body-image affects most women in our culture. Few women really *like* how we look and most of us spend huge amounts of money and time trying to get our appearance to conform to some socially acceptable — and totally unrealistic — ideal. In

Victorian times it was considered unladylike to eat heartily in public. Women also laced themselves into corsets so tight they displaced their vital organs and changed the shape of their bones. We think of them now as "old-fashioned," while we drug ourselves with diet pills, starve ourselves on grapefruit and black coffee and spend hours doing bizarre exercises which have little to do with maintaining good physical health. So much for change.

What we eat — and who gets to eat it — is also socially determined. In Kingston, 5,592 people asked for food from the Food Bank between 1985 and 1987. Of these, 50 per cent have been children and 41 per cent have been female-led families. In North America, the number of people who do not have enough to eat rises to millions. Most of these — the overwhelming majority — are women and children. As a society, we say we value children and women who care for them. But talk is cheap. Money, on the other hand, buys domed stadiums for men to play games in, not food.

Outside of North America, millions of people die daily from starvation. And here, too, the causes of their starvation are socially determined and very familiar. In many countries, land has been taken over for crops like cotton, coffee, carnations, and tobacco, which are aimed at North American markets. This leaves little good land on which to grow food. In order to survive, most people must work on the export plantation for wages *and* maintain a small plot to grow their own food as well.

In countries like Guatemala or El Salvador it is very often the women who work as low-wage workers on the plantations, forcing the men into the cities in search of other jobs. This situation, in addition to social custom, means that the women also maintain the small farm plots necessary to family survival.

In Africa, women produce approximately 80 per cent of the food grown on the continent. Many men, especially if wage-labor is not available, remain idle. A woman in Zaire may spend up to 8 hours a day in the fields, traveling up to 10 kilometres from her home. On her way back, she will carry a load of firewood weighing 30 or 40 kilos. She will also have to carry water several times a day, usually in calabashes weighing up to twenty kilos, from a source which is often four kilometres away.

Although they produce a large proportion of their country's food, women in Third World countries don't get to eat it. From the time they are weaned, girls generally receive less food than the boys; less food, in fact, than they need to develop normally. The result is a cycle of malnutrition in which young, undernourished mothers give birth to small babies whom they cannot adequately nurse. Complications of pregnancy and childbirth are the most common cause of death in women under 45 in developing countries. Half of these are associated with preventable undernutrition.

Of course, the practice of feeding women less is not peculiar to developing countries. In North American families too, women often eat less — or less wholesomely — than men. Sometimes they are forced to do this by husbands who control the family income; sometimes they are coerced by more subtle, but equally dangerous social pressures which urge women to be self-sacrificing.

Like women here, women in other countries are working to change their situation. In countries like Nicaragua, women are heavily involved in literacy campaigns, in the building of local health clinics, and in regaining land for co-operative use rather than export production. Projects like these are often the target of Contra attacks. Elsewhere, women are working to change a system of development aid, which, by concentrating on high technology, generally male-centered projects, often increases, or at best does not change, women's exploitation.

For the next few weeks, those of us who celebrate Christmas (and those of us who don't) will be deluged with images of feasting and plenty. And the dominant icon everywhere will be that of a mother and her child. The feasting and the plenty, in fact, are meant to convey the idea that the birth of a child is an event to celebrate.

On this planet, however, that is not always so. The politics of everyday demand that we ask certain questions. Questions like: whose child? Born where? A boy or a girl? Will she have enough to eat? Why not?

■ ■ ■ ■ ■

The Self-Perception of Girls:
Good Social Skills but Feelings of Inadequacy

"Girls need to realize and be taught to respect themselves for who and what they are and that they are worth something."

That statement, by a 13-year-old girl, speaks directly to what girls today do not realize and are not taught by the culture they live in. It comes from a survey conducted by Big Sisters of London as part of a wider examination of the needs of girls. The results of the survey indicate that we are failing our female citizens, miserably, just when they need us most.

The 93-item survey was designed to elicit information from girls on self-esteem, perception of control, physical competency, physical self-image, eating habits, cognitive clarity, relationships, skills, and values. It was given to a cross-section of girls and young women, after lengthy consultation with a pre-test group to ensure that the language and language-patterns used were appropriate to young girls. In addition, an informant group of 16- to 18-year-olds was established to compare and discuss the 13-year-old experience described in the survey.

Two hundred and sixty-one 13-year-olds and sixty-three 16- to 18-year-olds participated in the survey. In both cases, the survey was followed by group discussion. Four general areas emerged as focal points for discussion: strengths, body image, careers and occupations, competency and control. Here are some of the findings:

STRENGTHS: Repeatedly, girls indicated that their greatest strengths were in interpersonal and social skills, or skills that serve others. They valued being a good friend, being able to talk through problems, being fun to be with, and being honest. They indicated a desire to achieve and excel in school when they are supported and encouraged. They expressed the need to talk about the personal relevance of the topics they studied and to work out solutions through interaction.

In a previous essay I discussed the findings of another survey which examined how girls were treated in the classroom. In that survey, it was noted that questions and discussion were directed at boys more frequently than at girls and that boys' experience was more often the topic of discussion. It is important to remember, too, that our school system is one in which competition for high marks is accepted and valued, whereas working out solutions through interaction or sharing of information is often discouraged. It is little wonder that, despite their ability to list their strengths, girls indicated feelings of inadequacy and "not fitting in."

BODY IMAGE: 64 per cent of the participants in this survey had dieted by age 13; 30 per cent had used drastic measures such as drugs, laxatives, vomiting, etc. Yet only 30 per cent of the 13-year-olds and 41 per cent of the 16- to 18-year-olds actually saw themselves as overweight. In addition, the girls' perception of "overweight" was measured against an extreme of slimness, expressed as the ideal. It is important to remember, as well, that studies of teenage eating disorders have noted attendant psychological conditions such as low self-esteem, a feeling of not being in control of one's life, problems of identifying with being female. In addition, 74 per cent of those who reported dieting by age 13 also noted that the hardest thing for them to do is "deal with worries and fears."

Connected to body-image is the fact that the three highest-ranking activities among teenage girls were listed as talking on the phone, talking about my problems, just hanging around. Sports and other physical activities got low priority, a finding which matches the sharp decline of girls participating in such activities at this age. At the same time, the girls indicated a need for unconditional support and encouragement in order to engage in physical activities. As well, they talked about needing higher expectations from adults in order to develop physical skills.

I find this last particularly interesting, since it indicates that here

— as well as in intellectual activities — girls are picking up the message that not much is expected of them (except to be slim and pretty) and they are acting in accordance with that social expectation.

CAREERS AND OCCUPATIONS: "Choosing a career" was listed as the second hardest thing to do, just after dealing with worries and fears. The survey also showed that autonomy, competency, and achievement were among values least held by girls; the lowest value was put on being "smart" and "good at doing many different things." If we put this together with what girls saw as their strengths, we realize that girls need other reasons to achieve than simply success itself. Girls who were high achievers, in fact, indicated receiving support and encouragement from others. Other studies (notably Carol Gilligan's *In A Different Voice*) have also noted that girls do not value success and achievement at the expense of interpersonal relationships. While it is important that girls develop the necessary self-esteem to become high achievers, the results of this survey also indicate to me that we need to re-examine the highly competitive, success-at-any-cost value so prevalent in our culture.

The 13-year-olds also chose traditional occupations: fashion, teaching, animal care, clerical, dancing, nursing, counseling. There were some choices for things like "assistant scientist" or "assistant to lawyer," which also say a great deal about how girls see themselves. Also indicative of girls' sense of themselves is the fact that 27 per cent of the 13-year-olds and 43 per cent of the 16- to 18-year-olds expected that they would be doing something other than what they wanted by age 29. There is in these figures a sense of hopelessness which I find very depressing, especially since recent publications by the Ontario Ministry of Education indicate that this is a realistic reflection of the future for girls.

CONTROL AND COMPETENCY: While girls are very confident of their ability to interact positively with others, including teachers, they have little confidence about their academic skills. In addition, they do not take credit for the success they do achieve. In the 13-year-old group, 38 per cent attributed success to an external factor (I was lucky, the teacher liked me) while 58 per cent of the 16- to 18-year-old group did so. Other studies indicated that this dissociation, which may be linked with learned helplessness and perception of not being in control, is recognizable as early as ages 10 or 11.

The results of this survey should no longer be surprising or shocking. Once again it indicates that fully one half of our children are not developing the skills they need to achieve success in this culture and that the skills they do have are not valued. This situation has little to do with some genetic makeup in girls themselves and a great deal to do with their attempts to fit some socially-sanctioned ideal of femininity.

In response to the question "What would you tell a younger girl she needs to know?" the most frequent among the older group and the second most frequent among the younger was: "She needs to know how to stick up for herself."

If we wonder what our daughters need from us, we can't get it much plainer than that. When are we going to start listening?

■ ■ ■ ■ ■

Shaping a Young Male Mind

My son started back to school today. As I watched him race off, so nonchalantly, on his 10-speed, I felt that familiar mixture of longing and relief. Longing, because he has grown so fast, because he is only with me for such a short, short time; relief because the house is empty again, at last; I can have that second cup of coffee in peace and start work on the new story that's been filling my brain with its insistent racket.

But there was something else as well, another feeling, harder to define. My son is 13 now. More and more he looks to his peers and to grown men to teach him what he needs to learn about being a man in this culture. And as I watch him, watching the men who will be his role model, I wonder what he is seeing there.

I know what I *hope* he's learning and so, for the first day of school, I've prepared a sort of wish-list, especially for the mothers of sons.

In school, first of all. I know that in history class he will learn of the Great Heroes of his sex who founded colonies and fought wars to protect them, but I hope he learns, too, that the men who chose *not* to fight were heroes as well, not cowards or wimps. And I hope he learns a little of what the women were doing all this time, that someone besides me reinforces the ideas that the history of the spinning wheel is as important as that of the rifle.

And in English class, whose stories will he hear? Will all the central characters be boys, having adventures? Or will there be girls as well, strong, active girls who like to climb trees and solve mysteries as much as some of their brothers like to stay home and paint pictures?

My son has already told me that one of the most important aspects of his education so far has been the opportunity to learn another language. He has enjoyed his bilingual program and he wants to continue it. I hope he'll be able to. I hope his perception — that learning French *increases* his appreciation of English because it increases his appreciation of language in general — is one that teachers and administrators listen to. I hope he's not a victim of the kind of bigotry that sees the wider understanding of another's culture as some sort of threat to one's own.

I'm glad to see that he already takes cooking and sewing as well as wood and metal working. *That's* an improvement, certainly, but I hope that in gym class he learns to dance as well as to play basketball. And in playing basketball, I hope he learns to play for the fun of it, without some coach always yelling at him to get out there and win.

In social and environmental studies, I hope he learns to look critically at the society around him, to compare the role it offers him with the one it offers the girl who sits beside him and ask Why? I hope he learns to see the family as a basic unit in society, but one which is capable of infinite variety and change, just as the people who compose it are.

I hope he learns, too, that he lives on a very, very small planet, that he is one human being among billions, who, in turn, are only one species among millions and that his survival depends on his seeing this fact as a matter of *relationship* and not of domination.

In math and science class, I hope he learns that not everything can be quantified, measured, weighed. I hope someone points out to him that our society's belief in "objectivity" is a false one and that even to the so-called "hard sciences" we bring the biases of culture, class, and gender which determine, even when we don't recognize it, how and what we "see."

In every class, I hope he learns to listen to what the girls have to say as carefully as he listens to the other boys. I hope he learns that "conversation" carries within it the meaning of exploring ideas *together*, rather than that of mounting a debate in which only one point of view can "win."

But having gone to school myself, I know, of course, how much is *not* learned in the classroom, but in the playground, in the parks, on the street. Will there be men around to show him that the rough, aggressive comradeship that men so often employ is not the only way to express affection? I hope there are some to teach him that you can tell someone you love him by hugging him, as easily as by punching him on the arm or playing a practical joke. I also hope that if he worries that such an act might label him as a "sissy" or a "homo," someone will challenge him with "so what?"

And when he learns the insults of the playground, will someone point out to him that calling someone a "fag" is no different than calling someone a "nigger" or a "dago?"

And what about anger? Will there be enough examples besides what he has at home to counterbalance the pressure of a culture which accepts aggression and violence at every level as the only practical means of resolving conflict?

Every parent knows, of course, that there is only so much you can do. After that, you have to trust that you have done a good job. But for women like myself, who are the mothers of sons, this trust is a little harder to come by. Beyond the influence of our home, my son feels the enormous pressure of a culture which has a lot invested in the continuation of a traditional male role, a culture which offers enormous power and privilege to those who accept that limited idea of what it means to be a man.

As I watched my son ride off this morning, I realized that I was entrusting him to a public education system in its widest possible sense. What sort of man he becomes depends not only on his teachers, but also on everyone he meets, on how much they have thought about the roles our culture gives them depending on their sex and on how hard they work at changing those roles. Like every child, my son represents the future, but it's a future that grows out of our present. His limitations or possibilities, the possibilities for all of us, depend on what *we* do, now.

■ ■ ■ ■ ■

Before We Teach Sex to Children Let's Explore Our Own Feelings

In Monty Python's *The Meaning of Life* there's a very silly scene in which John Cleese plays an English schoolmaster teaching a sex education class. Since this is Monty Python, though, what this amounts to is the schoolmaster having sex with his wife in front of the class while describing, in emotionless terms, the physical aspects of what he is doing. The class, of course, goes on throwing spit balls and passing notes and not paying attention, so that the schoolmaster must, in the middle of "the act," summon people to the front of the classroom to hand out detentions.

The rest of this particular Monty Python movie was not particulary memorable, but this scene stayed in my mind as a perfect satire of how sex education is handled in our culture. And I think there's a connection between how we handle sex education and the popularity of pornography.

A lot of sex education programs — particularly those carried out in our schools — are basically courses in human plumbing. Students get a general idea of what goes where, some information about birth control and sexually-transmitted diseases, some talk about "responsibility," and that's about it. The one thing that isn't talked about is the one thing that motivates most of us to engage in sex in the first place: pleasure. Eroticism. Enjoyment. This is the aspect of sex education that we leave to magazines like *Playboy* and *Hustler*.

And these magazines do an excellent job. The women in the pictures look as if they're having a great time. The letters describe experiences that you won't find in any of those pamphlets in the guidance office at school and people manage to twist themselves into positions far more interesting than what Mr. (or Ms.) X described so haltingly in class last week. No wonder these magazines calculate that the majority of their sales are to young men.

Young women are another matter, of course. They're left with little useful information about their own sexual feelings while trying to sort through the web of often dangerous lies that magazines like *Playboy* perpetrate. Books like Alice Munro's *Lives of Girls and Women* or Margaret Laurence's *The Diviners*, which attempt to deal forthrightly with female sexual experience, are often banned from their schools or at least not taught in their English classes. Instead, they can read *Lord of the Flies* where a group of British schoolboys runs wild on a deserted island and end up killing each other with rocks.

This is real life. No wonder that Monty Python's satire pales by comparison.

What would I like to see in an ideal sex education course? As much information as possible, certainly, but by that I don't mean necessarily quantity. For me, preparing children for adulthood involves providing them with *a language and a context* in which to talk about sexual feelings. It means helping them to recognize that feelings are seldom about one simple thing and that sexual feelings in particular can involve a confusing complexity of lust and possessiveness, romantic love, hurts and rejection, anger and the desire to hurt back. We can't tell them what to do with these feelings, but we can give them the benefit of our culture's literature which is rich in stories of different kinds of love.

And I don't just mean those good old high-school classics like *Romeo and Juliet* or *Wuthering Heights* either. Besides the Munro and the Laurence already mentioned, there are Isabel Huggan's *The Elizabeth Stories*, or Lorna Crozier's funny, erotic poems entitled "The Sex Lives of Vegetables," or Raymond Carver's *What We Talk About When We Talk About Love*, which includes stories that deal with domestic violence, or Jane Rule's lesbian love story *Desert of the Heart*. There are lots of films too: Amy Heckerling's *Fast Times at Ridgemont High* has a lot to say about the sexual pressures teenage girls experience as does Bruce Beresford's *Puberty Blues*. Any mainstream film — *That Was Then, This Is Now* or *Pretty in Pink* — can provide the basis for a discussion, as could a Harlequin Romance or a series of episodes from a popular soap opera.

I also recognize that it's idealistic to expect that all of this will happen in a classroom. Teenagers may not always want to discuss sexual matters with adults and school may not be the best place for such discussions anyway. But there's no reason why this material can't be available, along with other, explicit information about sex, in guidance offices. And why do we assume that public sex education can only happen in school *or* is only needed by teenagers? Public libraries, Ys, churches, and other public meeting places could be centers for discussion and would help to convey the idea that most adults in our culture need sex education, too. It's interesting, for example, that most of the educating around AIDS has gone on in the schools as if somehow the rest of us don't need it.

Indeed, much of the discussion about public education on AIDS has been a strong indicator of our need to rethink our cultural attitudes about sex. All too often discussion has been carried on in an atmosphere of fear and homophobia, emphasizing repression and denial. Yet, another way of educating about AIDS might be to see it as an opportunity to talk explicitly about a wide range of sexual practices (including, but not limited to, intercourse) and how they can be carried on in a safe, *enjoyable,* and caring manner. To argue, as many people have, that this explicitness has nothing to do with preventing disease is to deny once again the basic reality that human beings like sex and that any effective sex education program must begin with that fact.

Changing our present approach to sex education offers us a chance to ask ourselves if censorship is the only method we have for dealing with pornography, or if there are choices. For me, this means asking ourselves some serious questions about our own feeling about sex, about what we as adults still need to explore and learn. We need to ask ourselves what we have to share with our children in this area and what possibilities there are for exploring some issues together. Beyond that are the explorations our children must continue on their own. What stories can we give them? What language can we offer?

As it stands, we offer a situation where explicit public service announcements about AIDS were considered too "offensive" for public TV, while commercials where teenage girls are used provocatively to sell chocolate bars and blue jeans are deemed okay. We offer a public education program which is all too often simplistic and boring. Then we let the pornographers do the rest.

■ ■ ■ ■ ■

The Evil of Family Violence Is Perpetuated When We Ignore Its Child Victims

A group of four-year-olds is playing house in the "kitchen corner" of a large play space. The little girl who is "mommy" wants to do the dishes.

Everyone helps her pile them in the sink and the game goes on until a story is suggested. The other children leave the dishwashing to listen.

"Don't you want to hear the story?" someone asks the little girl.

"No," she answers, "I have to get the dishes done or my husband will beat me when he gets home."

At four, this little girl is playing out what she knows of family life. Daddies beat mommies for not doing the dishes. And given the statistics on family violence, her remark could have been heard in many classrooms or day-care centers across the country. As it was, she happened to be in the play space at Kingston Interval House, a shelter for battered women and their children in Ontario.

Darlene George, the child support worker there, heard what she said and her response was to suggest that everyone play house. She became the "daddy" and started helping with the dishes. Two little boys got the ironing board out. Someone else began setting the table. Pretty soon the little girl stood back from the game, watching with interest.

"She was seeing something different," Darlene says, "another way of being a family that wasn't in her experience."

Darlene is one of two child support workers connected with Kingston Interval House; another works with the Community Support Program. Until a year ago, Darlene was one of three child support workers connected to shelters in eastern Ontario. Now, seven of the nine shelters employ them.

This change reflects a growing recognition that children are often the forgotten victims of family violence. Not only are they frequently yelled at and assaulted, they also learn very negative lessons on how to be adults themselves. People like Darlene see the results of these lessons: girls like the one in the story who assume that violence is normal and who have already accepted a victim position; boys who use aggression to resolve conflicts and who often assault their mothers while still in their early teens.

While these children are staying at Interval House, Darlene does what she can to help them talk about their feelings, to show them alternatives. She tries to do this gently, through play and story reading. There are a number of excellent books, written for children, about domestic violence. *Something's Wrong at My House* has strong pictures and two texts: one line for pre-schoolers and a longer piece for older children. *Mommy and Daddy Are Fighting* is aimed at 6-8 year olds; *I Love My Daddy But . . .* is set up like a coloring book, with large, simple pictures and text that deal with a child's experience of going to a shelter.

Such books are part of a growing emphasis on preventive education which Darlene feels is essential. The Kitchener-Waterloo school board, for example, has made discussion of family violence part of the curriculum for all grade-levels. I'd like to see it happening everywhere. Such an approach gives children information about alternatives. Children in violent situations have little opportunity to learn that what is happening to them is not what all families experience. Once they see that there are other possibilities, they may try to ask for help.

And this, in many ways, is where the larger tragedy begins. In all the books on domestic violence for children, the message comes across clearly: tell someone if you need help. But too often, children who do tell are not believed. This is a society in which children's perceptions are often devalued or laughed at. It's also a society in which many people cling so hard to the rosy ideal of the happy family that they won't believe anything else. So children remain the victims with the fewest options — and we all help to guarantee that the violence they learn will be continued through another generation.

Legally, professionals such as teachers are required to report students' stories of sexual or physical abuse to the Children's Aid Society. A caseworker who handles public education for that organization, emphasizes how important that is. "Abuse is seldom an isolated incident," he says. "It's an ongoing situation if it's kept a secret."

He also points out that reporting means help for the whole *family*, not necessarily punitive action. There are lots of resources available, and the emphasis is on helping people find alternatives to violent behavior, rather than simply removing children from their homes.

Most of us would call the police if we saw someone vandalizing our neighbor's car. How many of us would do something if we saw or heard our neighbor beating his wife? What about either parent hitting their children?

All too often, too many of us do nothing. We *say* this is because we "don't want to interfere," but what does "not interfering" *mean*? I think it means that we condone the right of men to use violence to control their wives and of parents to use violence to control their children. I think it means we're prepared to let this continue, rather than question our beliefs about the family, even as we say that the family is the most important unit in society.

Domestic violence is one of the most widespread crimes in our society. We know it can occur in any family, regardless of class, race, religion, or education level. It continues because we allow it to continue. That also means that we can change it. We can make sure there is wide public education about domestic violence, especially in the schools, and generous funding for shelters and programs for batterers. But we need to change ourselves too. We need to look at the ways in which we all use violence — or the threat of violence — to resolve conflict and try to change that. If we need help, we need to ask. And we have to find ways to offer help to others.

If you think there's something wrong next door, find an opportunity to ask. Sometimes a question like "Is there anything wrong at home?" can encourage a woman or a child to talk. Maybe not the first time you ask, but eventually. By asking you are also breaking down the isolation that often surrounds domestic violence and you are saying that the victims don't have to tolerate it. And listen to what children tell you, too. Report any stories of physical or sexual abuse to the appropriate child protection agency.

The widespread incidence of domestic violence is a message that we have to re-examine some of our ideas about the family. When Darlene George says, "What happens to these kids is more important than the privacy of the family," I agree with her. Completely.

■ ■ ■ ■ ■

A Story of Incest: Coping with Parents' Betrayal and Surviving the Damage

"In public my parents were really normal people. My father was a church elder. He was always really nice to people and they liked him. Then as soon as the door was closed, he'd turn into a monster. We grew up comfortably hating him."

Sarah is in her forties now and her words, like her face, seem calm as she tells her story. For you, too, reading them on this page, they will seem straightforward enough. You won't hear the undercurrent of pain and anger in her voice or see the effort it takes her to keep her face smooth. But I hope you will believe me when I tell you that as I sat listening to Sarah, I could hear in her voice the voice of the child she had been as if she were right there in the room, as if all the telling and re-telling would never completely heal the damage that had been done to her.

Sarah is an incest survivor. The word "survivor" rather than "victim" is important here, for though Sarah has been damaged, a large part of her story is about how she survived, how she fought back. "In the long run," she says, "in terms of the damage that's been done, that's been really important."

It's important, too, to understand that Sarah's family appeared to be a "normal" one. Her father was considered a "nice man." Like other forms of violence and abuse, incest is widespread and occurs in all kinds of families. Part of the damage done to its victims is that we like to think that it isn't so. When they try to tell us differently, we don't believe them.

This was Sarah's experience. It was also her sister's. When the latter was 15, their father tried to rape her. When she told their mother, she was thrown out of the house. Sarah was never told why her sister was sent away; she assumed she'd been "bad." It wasn't until much later that she learned the truth.

Sarah talks of her family as a place where "boys were the real people." Her father's rule was absolute. Her parents' marriage was not a good one. "They stayed together for the sake of the children," Sarah says, though her mother had frequent nervous breakdowns and was often in hospital. Sarah was expected to do all of the housework as well as care for her two younger brothers. Her father never displayed any affection to any of his children. "I was a very lonely kid, unloved by any parent. I was desperate for affection."

When Sarah was 14 and her mother was once again in hospital, her father suddenly began to be kind to her. "He took me skating and we did other things together. He never gave this love to any of us before. I wanted to believe in it. I wanted to have a real father."

What happened, however, was that her father began to kiss and fondle her in ways which she knew were wrong. "It was as if, since force didn't work with my sister, he was going to try kindness with me. It's horrifying to think he planned this. For years, my sense of betrayal was very strong."

Sarah finally told a friend, whose father was a chief of police with the Ontario Provincial Police. The father insisted that she tell her mother. "She just sat there like a stone; she made no response though she was clearly angry at me. I still expected support from her even though there was no concrete expression. I believed in the social image of mothers."

The police gave Sarah's father a warning, though not before they had questioned her about "what I was wearing, how I walked, whether I'd led him on." The result of the police action was a beating from her father, but the damage from the questioning went even deeper. Like many incest victims, Sarah had a strong sense that somehow some of this was her fault.

Shortly after this, she went to the Children's Aid asking for help, but their response was that there were no homes. "A large part of everyone's reaction, though, was that he hadn't actually succeeded. Since my father hadn't completed intercourse with me, everyone seemed to assume that I obviously hadn't been hurt."

Sarah left home the day she turned 16 and shortly after married "the boyfriend of the moment." "In a way," she says, "it was a survival tactic." When that relationship became abusive, she left. By now, she had two young children. She still went home to visit, though she never spoke to her father. The rest of the family ignored this.

While her children were still small, Sarah managed to go back to school, get an education, and find a good job. It was only when her younger brother committed suicide, when she was 29, that she began to deal openly with the incest. "In some ways I felt I had abandoned my brother to that suicide. I knew I had to start dealing with what had happened to me."

As she began to talk about it, Sarah found that some of her friends had had similar experiences; she began to read feminist literature and to get involved in the feminist movement. She began to hear other women's stories, especially as she started working at the Sexual Assault Crisis Center. This was important in her own healing. "As you're training yourself not to blame other victims, you're also learning not to blame yourself."

She has also worked hard at her mothering skills, at "not passing on the damage." She has three birth children and has also provided a home for several foster children. And she has had to deal with her own mother's complicity in what happened. "For a long time I thought my father was the only villain. I couldn't cope with my mother's betrayal. For a long time, I thought I must have misunderstood her or, worse, that I must be really awful if my own mother didn't like me."

Sarah calls this "motherism," that strong need we have to believe our culture's ideology about the nature of mothers, just as we need to believe in the myth of the happy family. As she sees it, these myths do a lot of damage to the victims of violence and abuse. A big part of her own progress was cutting herself off completely from her family. When her mother died, she felt only immense relief. While she recognizes that she did all she could as a child to change her situation, she also feels that "a big part of my problem was that no one actively helped me. They seemed content to leave these people in charge of my life."

Sarah believes that we can't do much about incest unless we are prepared to offer children alternatives. She notes that in Sweden children can leave home and live elsewhere with public support. She would like to see similar group homes here. Obviously, this means seeing children as independent citizens and not as the possessions of their parents. Once again, it means looking at our most cherished beliefs about the family.

Sarah also talks about the importance of explicit sex education in dealing with incest. "If we're going to talk about sexual abuse we have to talk about sex first. Part of my problem was that I didn't really have the words for what was happening to me. The silence around sexual information contributes directly to abuse."

Sarah is a survivor. She has used her own damage creatively to change the situation for others, but she also recognizes that dealing with what has happened to her will take the rest of her life. Although she is now in a safe and loving relationship, for example, she still has sexual problems. She's tried various sex therapies, but none of them have helped her. What does help is marijuana, which allows her to relax so that she can enjoy sex. "Someday I hope not to have to, but at the same time, I can't imagine men saying they'd rather go without orgasm than not smoke dope." Sarah feels that this is important information for other incest survivors as well and she asked me explicitly to mention this.

At first I was worried this one detail would discredit everything else in her story, though I realize that such an attitude is hardly a tribute to you as a reader. And it also says a great deal about me as a writer, about my desire to give you only superwomen in these essays, women who've worked things out in ways that even my grandmother would approve of. But we all know that Superwoman is as much a myth as the Perfect Mother and the Always-Happy Family. The reality is each of us working through the damage we have suffered as best we can, sharing our stories as openly as possible in the hope that even the smallest details may be of use.

That's what I love and admire about Sarah. That's what I trust you to remember.

■ ■ ■ ■ ■

Women Speak Out to Women: A Heartbreaking Record of Painful Experience

Sunday afternoon. About 40 women gather in the church hall at St. Paul's. The seats have been set up to form a sort of lopsided circle, half of which contains several chairs, arranged in three semi-circular rows. The other half is made up of only seven chairs and these remain empty until 2 o'clock. Then, seven very nervous-looking women take their places. The Take Back the Night Speak Out is about to begin.

During the next two hours the room fills up with words, with stories, with names, with the sound of women crying, and with the tense laughter that sometimes grows out of nervousness and pain.

Joanne McAlpine, director of Kingston Interval House, reads a list of women's names. Sandra. Tammy. Janice. Julie. Erica. All women who, in the last few months, have been murdered by their husbands or boyfriends.

Another woman talks of being sexually abused as a child by the landlord and when she told her mother, being warned not "to give the guy a hassle" because it was hard to find a place to live.

Pat describes sitting in her family living room with her brother and sisters listening while her father dragged her alcoholic mother into the basement and smashed a liquor bottle into her face to "beat some sense into her" about her drinking.

"I used to go downstairs and knock on the door until my knuckles bled," she sobs, "hoping he'd stop, but he never did. I was so helpless."

Cynthia talks about how she "married a nice guy," and had a good marriage until she became pregnant. After that her husband became angry and abusive, slapping her frequently and destroying her personal property. She finally left him after he beat her while she was holding their newborn son. "There was blood all over," she tells us, "my only thought was that my baby and I were going to die together."

Linda describes being assaulted at 15 when she took a ride with a stranger, shortly after moving to a larger center from a rural community. "I was so naive," she says, "I didn't know about strangers. So I thought what happened was all my fault."

"What happened" was that the man drove to a deserted park, held her down in the seat, locked the doors, and rammed his fingers into her vagina. "I knew enough to know this wasn't exactly rape, but I didn't know what I would call it. In 1978, you didn't call it anything." After the incident, Linda did not tell anyone, though she attempted suicide twice. In fact, although she has worked with sexual assault victims herself for some time, she did not talk about her own experience until this summer. "I'm doing this today," she says, "because I want people here to know that his happens to real people, people that you know."

Lisa describes being forced to masturbate a male babysitter when she was nine and then to perform oral sex on a school janitor when she was 11. After this second incident, she started drinking and for many years, used alcohol as a way of blocking her pain. She finally went to a counselor, but even in that situation she admits that she was just "talking and thinking." She was afraid to feel.

"I used to call it 'falling apart,' " she says. "It took years of hard work to get to the point where I started to *feel* it wasn't my fault. Most days now I can say 'I like you' to myself. I'm working on 'I love you.' "

None of these stories comes easily. There are long silences in which the women struggle with their tears or search for words. But though these silences are tense and uncomfortable, they also carry within them a kind of power. It is as if every woman in the room recognizes that this is not the kind of silence which has defeated and separated us for so long. This is not a silence which denies our stories, but one which gives us time to gather the strength to continue telling them.

The circle is part of this strength too. Those of us who listen face those who speak, but there is no artificial division between "audience" and "expert." Instead, in the circle, there is a recognition that the women who are telling their stories today are speaking for all of us, just as the circle draws us all together. As one woman said: "Every woman is an expert on violence against women."

The Speak Out was the opening event for the Take Back the Night Week, which also included educational events, a march through the city streets, and a women's dance. The advertising pamphlet called it "a week of education, protest, celebration." I like that. I like the recognition that the three are inextricably connected. I also believe that the Speak Out makes those connections real.

The stories the seven women tell are seven more versions of a story that many, many women have told. In speaking they not only educate those who listen, they also add their voices to those of other women who refuse to be silent any longer. In doing so they break more than silence. They break the myths our culture has constructed to blame women for rape and violence, to make us responsible for what we wear and how we act and where we go at night, rather than expecting the men who commit these crimes to change.

And those of us who listen realize, as we sit in the circle, that this is our story too, that what happens to any one woman affects us all, that what joins us together is the fact that, in this culture, *all* women are in danger because we are women.

The power of something like a Speak Out lies in the way it connects the personal experience of individual women to the political context in which it happens. Instead of experts (or party candidates) telling us what the issues are, each woman speaks from her own pain and is believed by those who hear her. In speaking out, we discover what we share. And in discovering what we share, we discover the power to heal our pain, by working together to change the society that causes it.

That's what we have, always, to celebrate.

Violence: A One-Way Street Leading Nowhere

"It's like having a toolcase with only one tool. If all you have is a hammer, you go around hammering things. If you get a screwdriver, you have other options."

No, Rick is not giving me a quick course in carpentry. He's talking about emotions. About how, if anger is the only emotion you know how to express, it ends up running your life. Too often, it leads to violence. Rick should know. He used to batter his wife.

Wife beater. Having worked at Interval House, I wasn't sure I wanted to meet Rick. I'd seen too many bruises, too many frightened eyes. When I knocked on the door, I half expected to see a monster.

What I saw was a slim man in his early 40s, a man with regular white-collar job and a growing business of his own. He had kind eyes and a pleasant manner. In other words, your ordinary North American male.

And that's the point. Most batterers are not monsters or "sickos"; they're simply men who've been brought up in a culture where our expectations of what "being a man" is all too often leads to violence.

"It's hard being a male and having all kinds of pressure in your life you don't even know exist. Men have no opportunity to acquire knowledge about their emotions. We don't even know what emotions there are. You come home from work after a bad day and start screaming at everyone 'Don't bother me!' because you can't come in and say, 'Look, I feel bad. Somebody hurt my feelings. Can we talk about it?' Being a man means being in control. You can be happy or you can be angry. That's it."

Rick's story is typical of many men who batter. I've changed his name, but the words and the events are his.

Like many batterers, Rick grew up in a violent home. His father beat his mother and he himself was often physically abused. He assumed this went on in most families. "When you're a kid you auto-matically assume your parents are okay."

Rick's first marriage, at 21, was not physically violent, though he admits he was psychologically abusive. It was during his second mar-riage that he began to beat his wife. "It came out under certain condi-tions, not being able to control a situation, believing that the male role is to be the master of the house."

Like many men in his situation, Rick had very traditional, stereo-typical ideas of men's and women's roles in marriage. His role meant "I had to know where she was all the time. I had to be the white knight that saved her from everything." Naturally, such unrealistic expectations for himself made him "tremendously insecure." But since feeling insecure was not an emotion he could admit, what came out were anger and violence.

Afterwards "I felt really bad. Disappointed in myself, tremendously so. I didn't seem to know of any other options. I felt, God this is the only way I know how to deal with this . . . I didn't have any respect for my wife. I thought of her as a fool, just a woman or whatever. She became 'the bitch.' "

But then ". . . one day I was sitting in the den. It had a folding wooden door. I remember I went into a real rage and I grabbed the door off the hinges, threw it on the ground and started jumping up and down on it with my fists clenched. Suddenly I saw myself . . . I saw this raging gorilla and it scared the shit out of me. I thought, this is as low as I want to go. I thought, boy, you've got to change."

Not long after, Rick met a friend who told him he was going to Alternatives, a program for violent men. "I laughed and said, 'You mean you're violent.' As soon as I said that, I thought, you hypocritical bastard."

Because of his friend's comments, Rick contacted Alternatives. The program offers group work with other violent men to learn where anger comes from and how to control it. One-to-one counseling is also available. It wasn't easy. "But the first thing I learned at the group was that I wasn't the only one in the world. It was the first significant relief."

Rick now works as a volunteer with Alternatives himself. He has learned "how to handle things differently, to recognize the physical warning signs of a blow-up and deal with it at a less intense level. I feel more truly in control; I can say what I feel. Things don't have to get to the boiling point."

Rick's message to other men who are still being violent is: "Give yourself a break." And when he says it, it means so many things. Like not buying the roles our culture gives to men and women that cheat and limit us all. Like realizing boys can cry if they need to and that violence is a one-way street leading nowhere.

Like understanding that it's possible, always possible to change.

■ ■ ■ ■ ■

The Power of a Group of Mothers Getting Together 'Just to Talk'

When my son was born 14 years ago, I was living in a small apartment in Windsor. My partner was working as a postal clerk and because of his low seniority he was on permanent midnights. This meant we hardly ever saw each other, except briefly in the morning (he would be crawling into bed just as I got out of it), and even more briefly in the evenings, before I sank into the mind-numbing, speechless exhaustion of new mothers.

It meant, too, that I was home alone with our son much more than either of us had wanted. Alone and not alone. As the baby grew older and noisier, I had to keep him quiet while his father slept; by the time he was asleep and I was still awake enough to talk, his father was off to work. Things got even crazier when I had to go back to work after six months, first as a counselor in a women's center (where I could take my son with me), then to my former job as a secretary. Sometimes I went for days without seeing my partner. Weeks rushed together in a blur of alarm clocks, meals, day care, typewriters, errands, trips to the park, bills, groceries, and laundry, laundry, laundry.

This was not what I'd thought motherhood would be. None of the books I'd read prepared me for the nitty-gritty day-to-day of it, any more than they prepared me for the new emotions I was experiencing. How could I feel this angry, sometimes this frustrated, with someone I loved this much? How could I feel so helpless and afraid? Was I always going to be this tired? Any feminist perspective I'd had seemed to collapse with my ability to utter more than a few coherent sentences at any one time. And since I was one of the first of my group of friends to have a baby, I felt even more isolated and alone. I began to think I was a complete failure. I was falling apart.

Finally, I talked to another woman I knew casually, a woman with a four-year-old daughter. Her eyes filled with tears as she listened to me. "That's just how I feel," she cried. "It's crazy to think we've never talked about it. Or that we're the only ones."

And that's how it began, the group we called The Mother's Group. A few phone calls were all it took to pull together a group of 10 women. All were mothers; all were interested in getting together to talk.

We were an odd assortment. Our ages ranged from 19 to 40; our children's from newborn to teenage. Some of our husbands worked at the auto plants, some were professionals; some of us were on our own. We got together every other Thursday, no matter what. We shared tips and advice and children's clothes, we laughed and cried and argued and complained. We talked and talked and talked. That group saved my life and my sanity.

And its importance all came back to me, whole, when I attended a Mothers for Change meeting recently. Mothers for Change is a group that began two years ago with the North Kingston Community Development Project. Many of its members live in the area; several are single mothers on mother's allowance, but anyone is welcome.

Like my group, Mothers for Change is primarily a support group.

The group co-ordinator organizes speakers for some meetings — people to talk about raising adolescents, about eating well on a budget, about how to get ready for a job interview. Straightforward, practical information, in other words. But like my group too, it seems that these women learn most from each other.

"When I first started," one says, "I just came for something to do. I went home thinking I didn't have the problems some of the other women had, I didn't belong. But then I got to see them as friends. I learned to trust these women. Now, I get a lot out of it."

"If I'm depressed before I come here," says another woman, "I always come out of the group feeling better."

The day I was there, the talk drifted (as it always seems to do among women) from practical information about Mothers' Allowance, to dealing with kids, to one woman's story about how her daughter won the IDA Easter coloring contest, to plans for Mothers' Day. The group is going to treat themselves to lunch together for Mothers' Day, and there was some hope that a local florist would donate a rose for each of them. "We deserve a treat," someone said, and no one was about to disagree.

The group also involves itself in the community. For over a year now, Mothers for Change has run the free clothing drop-in located at Queen Elizabeth Collegiate and Vocational Institute. Clothing which is donated to the community development project is distributed free to people who need it. The group also provided information and personal experience for the play about single parents, *Solo Flight*.

At present, a second such group is being organized. It's going to be open to fathers as well as mothers and will be taking over the running of the clothing depot. Mothers for Change is planning new activities, such as spending time with elderly residents at nearby Providence Manor and Rideaucrest during the summer months. Both the new group and Mothers for Change are open to new members.

When I think back to my first months of motherhood, the feeling that I recall most clearly is one of isolation. Physical isolation, certainly, at home alone with a small child, cut off from the rest of the world. Emotional isolation, too, feeling that no other mother was ever as scared or as inadequate or as tired as I was. I know now that those feelings are common to many mothers, that they "come with the job" in many ways. And I learned that — not just my head, but in my heart — from The Mother's Group.

For me, this is the power that such groups have, the power that comes when a group of people get together "just to talk." In my case, that power has expressed itself in many ways. The women in my original group are still friends. Some of them have formed the Windsor Feminist Theater, working together to perform (and sometimes write) plays that explore women's experience. Others have gone back to school or found the courage to try new jobs. One of us attended the International Women's Conference in Nairobi in 1986. My own decision to take the plunge as a writer came, in part, from the strength I gained in that group.

"I was bored as hell at home," one of the women at the Mothers for Change meeting says, "but when I first came here, I thought I had nothing in common with the others."

"Yeah," another woman says to her, laughing. "But we slowly worked that off. Now we're working on your problems."

Everyone laughs and it's a laugh I recognize from my own experience. The laugh that comes when you look back at the woman you were before and see how scared you were at first, how alone. The laugh that means it's hard to believe how much you've changed, what a few hours over a coffee with a few women can do for your life. The laugh that says — hey, anything is possible, even for me.

■ ■ ■ ■ ■

An Auction at Mother's Childhood Home

Last week, my mother and I went to an auction sale in Enterprise, Ontario. It was one of many such sales I will attend this summer, though I seldom buy anything. I just like to look at the jumble of things — and I like to watch the auctioneers in action, their singsong patter one of the sounds that mean summer to me.

Last week's sale was no different than any other. There was the usual collection of everything from canning jars to double beds, a wonderful set of wicker lawn furniture, some beautiful old tools — you know, the sort of stuff that just seems to grow from 40-odd years of living in one place. And there was that strangely familiar silence in the empty house, as if the house itself were wondering what — or rather, who — would happen to it next.

This sale did have one major difference, though. The house we were visiting was the house my mother had lived in as a girl, the house where my father had courted her and where their wedding luncheon had been served after the ceremony. She took me through all the rooms, telling me how they had looked back then — my grandfather had sold the place 40 years ago — describing the views out the various windows, as she remembered them. We ran into old school chums of hers and the talk drifted, as it does among women, until various members of various families, their antecedents and connections, their current states of health, their children and grandchildren, were all satisfactorily accounted for.

It was strange to stand in that house, where I had never stood before, and to realize how little I knew of my mother's early life. My father's boyhood home is very familiar to me, as is his family. My mother's is not. Some of this, in my case, is simply a result of circumstance — my maternal grandmother died before I was born, whereas my father's mother lived until I was in my 20s. Both my grandfathers died when I was a child.

But there is a cultural factor here as well. In a patriarchy, the primacy of the father is taken for granted. And what this often means, in everyday life, is the loss of our mothers' families and our mothers' childhoods. It is a loss — or rather a renunciation — that is symbolized when a married woman takes her husband's name, a situation that, until recently, was assumed as a matter of course. It is also a loss that every woman I know speaks of — sometimes with bitterness and pain.

My first book of poems, *Marrying into the Family*, explored this loss in many ways. I began to write the poems in the first place because I was struck by how little I knew about any of my female ancestors. I was struck, too, by how many had died young, either in childbirth or from TB, and how quickly they had been succeeded by second wives, stepmothers. And since contact was not always maintained with the first wife's family, the natural, hereditary links seemed doubly lost to me.

"As a woman," writes poet Lorna Crozier in an essay, "I cannot take my mother's name, my mother has no name; as a woman, I cannot take my mother's country, my mother has no country. As a woman, my country has no name, my name is no one's country."

Often this loss includes the loss of material links as well. Many, many women I know, whose mothers have died, complain of losing precious reminders of her — dishes, furniture, jewelery — when their fathers remarry and these are taken over by his new wife. Under this grief is also a current of anger, too. Anger that the mother can be so easily replaced and all trace of her existence lost to her children.

This loss is compounded by the lack of information available to us about past women's lives. If I want to get a sense of my father's life, for example, I have lots of easily available books, movies, television programs. Not so my mother. One of the advantages of Women's Studies programs, and other sorts of feminist research, is that they act as reclamation projects, returning to us at least some of what has been lost.

We all begin with a mother. We all begin with a mother who is the center of our world, the most powerful person we know. It is amazing that so much power and importance can be lost so quickly or that it can come to be perceived only as negative, as when mothers alone are blamed for the failings of their children or when we speak disparagingly of someone who is "too close" to his or her mother.

Indeed, our culture has spent a lot of time finding ways to curtail the power of the mother. The increasing intervention of more and more technology in the birthing process is one example. The fate that many mothers meet in the courts is another. Phyllis Chesler's book *Mothers on Trial* provides excellent documentation for the numerous situations in which women lose custody disputes, often to abusive men, because they are seen to be "unfit" by patriarchal standards. Another way of "blaming mother." Or think of mother-in-law jokes, culturally accepted ways of diminishing her power.

And yet that power can never be entirely diminished. Even when men's lives and men's doings are the center of our culture, there are thousands of oblique, often subversive, references to the power of the mother. Indeed, it is almost as if these references have to be oblique in order not to be censored. Some feminist scholars argue that they are all that is left of a rich and complex matriarchal literature which we have lost.

Take *Cinderella* for example, one of the oldest fairy tales known. Like many of these tales, it comes from an ancient oral tradition and this particular story is known in many languages, including Chinese. In all versions, the presence of Cinderella's dead mother's spirit is remarkable. In the familiar Grimm version she is a little bird who lives in the tree which grows on her grave, and it is she who provides Cinderella with the clothes that she wears to the ball. In one sense, she is far more powerful than the prince, and it is by her power that Cinderella is delivered to a life of wealth and safety. It is interesting to note, too, that the stepmother, the usurper, is seen as "evil" in this tale because she shows no affection for another woman's child. The fact that all this power gets diminished, in the Walt Disney version, to a silly fairy godmother says a great deal.

This reading of Cinderella is only one, of course, but it's one to think about. Many feminists dismiss Cinderella as being only about how girls should grow up to marry princes. We must remember, first of all, that most of these tales have peasant origins and that, from the point of view, marrying a prince might be just fine. We might also re-read this tale — and others — to find out what it says about mothers and their power. Some scholars argue that earlier versions of these tales give even more power to the mother, power that has been curtailed in later, patriarchal versions.

Or think of stories like *Anne of Green Gables* and *Jane Eyre* in the light of what they say about the sorrow and dislocation of motherless children. And in the great southern black spiritual, "Sometimes I Feel Like a Motherless Child," the loss of the mother becomes a metaphor for the loss of a country, for being sold into slavery in an alien and hostile place.

In modern literature by women, the search for the mother and what she means is a constant theme. Grace Paley comes to mind, as does Jamaica Kincaid, Margaret Laurence, Adrienne Rich, and many, many others. I'll end with one of my favorite quotes from "The Ottawa Valley," a story by Alice Munro in which a woman remembers a journey she made, as a young girl with her mother, to her mother's birthplace. A story in which she tries to come to terms with everything her mother means to her and with her own conflicting feelings about her mother, feelings which, until recently, we have not been given the language to explore:

The problem, the only problem, is my mother. And she is the one of course that I am trying to get; it is to reach her that this whole journey has been undertaken. With what purpose? To mark her off, to describe, to illuminate, to celebrate, to get rid of her, and it did not work, for she looms too close, just as she always did. She is heavy as always, she weighs everything down, and yet she is indistinct, her edges melt and flow. Which means she has stuck to me as close as ever and refused to fall away, and could go on and on, applying what skills I have, using what tricks I know, and it would always be the same.

■ ■ ■ ■ ■

Points of View on the Work of Mothering

Now that the Mother's Day chocolates have been eaten and the roses are beginning to fade, those of us who actually are mothers are back to the wonderful, exasperating, crazy, complex, day-to-day *work* of mothering. This is a post-Mother's Day column. It's not as neat as a greeting card verse, but it tries to say something about the actual experience — from as many different points of view as possible.

British poet Jeni Couzyn first. This excerpt is from "Transformation," one in a series of poems about pregnancy and childbirth called "Life By Drowning":

I see you dart into the world
pearly pink like the inside of a shell
streaked with silver.
Look! Look!
I am shouting with joy, rising up
like a phoenix from my pain.

Some of the wonder in the love we feel for our children is expressed in these lines from a poem called "Reflection: Mother and Child," by Carolyn Smart:

He lies in my arms now wanting only my comfort,
I need him just as much, tomorrow again he'll push
apart from my life. In the slow evening's pause
the room is aglow with his face. I think of the days
before he was born: such ignorance! Then glance up
and see it, a reflection in the eastern window:
small child in some woman's arm. It's me
who once thought I was afraid to love as much as this.

But beside that love there are often darker, less expressed feelings. In Tillie Olsen's story "I Stand Here Ironing," a woman who has raised her children alone, in poverty, tries to explain her situation (in her imagination) to a teacher who has said that her child "needs help":

I will never total it all. I will never come in to say: She was a child seldom smiled at. Her father left me before she was a year old. I had to work her first six years when there was work, or I sent her home and to his relatives . . . We were poor and could not afford for her the soil of easy growth. I was a young mother. I was a distracted mother. There were other children pushing up, demanding . . . My wisdom came too late . . . . Let her be. So all that is in her will not bloom — but in how many does it? There is still enough left to live by. Only help her to know — help make it so there is cause for her to know — that she is more than this dress on the ironing board, helpless before the iron.

Some of this feeling is explored in another way in this passage from Adrienne Rich's powerful and important book *Of Woman Born*:

The physical and psychic weight of responsibility on the woman with children is by far the heaviest of social burdens. It cannot be compared with slavery or sweated labor because the emotional bond between a woman and her children make her vulnerable in ways which the forced laborer does not know; he can hate and fear his boss or master, loathe the toil; dream of revolt or of becoming a boss; the woman with children is a prey to far more complicated, subversive feelings. Love and anger can exist concurrently; anger at the conditions of motherhood can become translated into anger at the child, along with the fear that we are not 'loving'; grief at all we cannot do for our children in a society so inadequate to meet human needs becomes translated into guilt and self-laceration. This 'powerless responsibility' . . . is a heavier burden even than providing a living — which so many mothers have done, and do, simultaneously with mothering — because it is recognized in some quarters, at least, that economic forces, political oppression, lie behind poverty and unemployment; but the mother's very character, her status as a woman, are in question if she has 'failed' her children.

When Rich speaks of a society that is "inadequate to meet human needs," she is talking of *this* society, where the majority of those who live below the poverty level are women and children — and where the number of families who are homeless increases by the hour. That is part of motherhood, too.

On the desk beside me is a list of figures from a book called *The State of the World's Children*, published this year by UNICEF. The list is of the 64 countries with the highest infant and child mortality rates in the world. Places like Ethiopia, India, Egypt, Peru, Kenya, Zimbabwe, South Africa, and Nicaragua. The highest rate is 325 deaths (before age five) for every 1,000 births. The lowest is 95.

Many of these deaths are caused by the dehydration associated with malnutrition. Oral rehydration therapy is a simple procedure using water, salt, and sugar to prevent dehydration. This procedure could be made available to every needy child on the planet for the amount of money spent on pet food in the United States in one year. This is also part of motherhood.

So is the fact that the maternal mortality rate in Ecuador is 212 per 100,000 live births. In Kenya it is 204. In Canada, 17.

It is in this context that I remember these lines from Margaret Atwood's poem "Christmas Carols":

Children do not always mean
hope. To some they mean despair.
This woman with her hair cut off
so that she could not hang herself
threw herself from a rooftop, thirty
times raped and pregnant by the enemy

who did this to her. This one had her pelvis
broken by hammers so the child
could be extracted. Then she was thrown away,
useless, a ripped sack. This one
punctured herself with kitchen skewers
and bled to death on a greasy
oilcloth table, rather than bear
again and past the limit. There
is a limit, though who knows
when it may come?

The current state of the planet necessitates a dark side to motherhood which we ignore all too often. This next passage is from Germaine Greer's excellent book *Sex and Destiny*, one which I recommend to anyone who wishes to think seriously about motherhood and its related issues — reproductive freedom and abortion:

Sentimentalized notions of motherhood have blurred the real nature of the maternal function as it has been carried out since prehistory. In reality motherhood is a bloody business from the first menstruation through pregnancies, births, miscarriages, infant deaths and the frequent deaths of mothers themselves. Besides the virtues of tenderness, patience and self-forgetfulness, a mother had to exercise courage, determination and decisiveness. It was not only her duty to see that the number of children remained in the right balance with the adult population and the potential food supply. It was she who instructed her attendant not to wash the child that she had brought forth in pain, or to see that it did not draw its first breath. She herself may have bashed its brains out with a rock, or thrown it on the ground or against a tree, or strangled it with a vine or stood upon a stick laid across its neck or poured sand into its mouth. Such violent acts were the more merciful; the fate of children thrown into ditches or cesspits or left on hillsides to die of exposure was more cruel, as the people who gathered up the children of American soldiers from Vietnamese ditches can testify.

Those of us who find the idea of infanticide disgusting, uncivilized or sinful might remember that we allow infanticide every day. We allow it because we allow the conditions under which children here and elsewhere starve to death by the thousands, daily.

Or as Margaret Atwood puts it at the end of the poem I've already quoted from:

> If mother-
> hood is sacred, put
> your money where your mouth is. Only
> then can you expect the coming
> down to the wrecked & shimmering earth
> of that miracle you sing
> about, the day
> when every child is a holy birth.

■ ■ ■ ■ ■

Goddesses and Human Habits

Sometimes an idea for an essay simply falls into my lap. I was sitting at my desk the other day, and when I reached up to the bookshelf beside me for Volume II of my *Shorter Oxford Dictionary*, another book tumbled down with it: *The Woman's Encyclopedia of Myths and Secrets*. Compiled by Barbara G. Walker and published by Harper & Row, this thick book is as valuable to me as the *Oxford* and often for the same reasons.

The *Oxford* gives me the origins of words, tracing them back through their various usages and connotations to their earliest appearance in English. *The Woman's Encyclopedia* does much the same thing with myths, superstitions, folk songs, and scriptures. Only it traces many of these to their pre-patriarchal origins, exploring what the jacket calls the "thousand hidden pockets of history and custom." I've spent many an enjoyable hour with this book, just as I have with the *Oxford*, not looking for anything in particular, simply browsing. Today's browse uncovered the following:

Starting with the A's we have the apple, which was a fruit of mystic significance long before Eve took a bite. It has long been considered the goddess's sacred heart of immortality, grown in her many western paradises. The Celts called this paradise Avalon or "Appleland." The Scandinavians thought apples essentials to resurrection and placed them in graves, believing they carried the soul from one body to the next. The tradition of the yule pig with an apple in its mouth is also connected to these beliefs, since in the ancient Scandinavian cycle the boar-god was sacrificed at this time and the apple served as a heart in the next life. Slicing an apple transversely reveals the magic pentacle of Kore, the virgin manifestation of the goddess who is hidden in the heart of Mother Earth (Demeter), just as her sign is hidden in the heart of the apple.

A few pages further along we come to Cupid, the son of Venus and Mercury, the ancient symbol of sexual union. In Christian usage (and this might give us pause for thought) the ancient significance of sexual desire was confused with desire for money: thus the modern meaning of the word "cupidity" is greed; originally it meant lust. A similar misunderstanding of Cupid's full meaning is evident in the Renaissance artistic tradition of rendering him as a winged baby. Ancient talismans were a little more direct: winged phalli of bronze, ivory, or wood, which gave rise to an Italian slang term for the male genitalia, *ucello* or "little bird."

On page 508, we find that kissing, like many forms of affectionate contact, was an adaptation of primitive mother-child behavior. Many of our gestures of embrace began as imitations of the nursing mother and kissing may have originated with mouth-to-mouth feeding, the common practice of mothers offering their infants pre-chewed food. Kissing was most common in European countries, where it was supposed to create stronger bonds among clan members. Hence, perhaps, the term "kissing cousins." In many other cultures, particularly in northern Asia, the practice was unheard-of. Among Amerindians and Inuit, the custom was to inhale the breath of a loved one by rubbing noses.

Kissing sometimes leads to "tying the knot," an expression we still use for marriage. In the older religions, the Fate-goddess wove and tied together the threads of life. Marriage was viewed as the binding together (tying the knots of) two life threads by Aphrodite.

As might be expected, the *Encyclopedia* makes many references to the goddesses of ancient religions. These goddesses took many forms, of course, but the most common of these was that of the trinity or the Triple Goddess which included Virgin, Mother, and Crone in a single figure who held within her the power of life and death. In the ancient religions, Virgin, Mother, and Crone were seen as *inextricably* part of a whole which could not be understood outside of this relationship, though the goddess might appear in one or other of her manifestations at different times.

And the idea of the trinity has many representations — the three Fates of Greek tradition and the three "weird sisters" in Shakespeare's *Macbeth* are two examples, as are the continuous appearances in fairy tales of the old crone or wise woman whose advice saves the young princess. What has happened, of course, is that what was once seen as three manifestations of a single, powerful whole is now treated as three separate and often opposing "types." In the same way, many of our cultural representations of women perpetuate this either/or way of looking at things: women get to be either Good Girls or Bad Girls, Virgins or Whores, for example. What we have lost is a view of woman in which youth, sexual activity and mothering, aging and death are all seen and celebrated as part of a whole person.

It would be easy enough to look somewhat askance at my *Woman's*

Encyclopedia, to question its sources and to present contradictory evidence for some of its interpretations. But that seems to me to be a rather limiting exercise. So much of what we know about any other area of human experience — history, anthropology, sociology, religion — has to do as much with the interpretation of certain data as with the facts themselves. What I like about the encyclopedia is that it offers both new information and a new way of looking at information I already have.

All of which brings me to *widdershins* — or *withershins*, if you will. My trusty *Shorter Oxford* gives as the meaning of this adverb: "1. In a direction opposite to the usual; the wrong way"; and "2. In a direction contrary to the apparent course of the sun (considered as unlucky or causing disaster)." Interesting, isn't it? Why is a "direction opposite to the usual" suddenly the "wrong one"? And who considers it "unlucky"?

Here's what my equally trusty *Woman's Encyclopedia* has to say: "Counterclockwise, the direction of the moon or 'left-hand path' of pagan dances (still prevalent in folk tradition). To open the door of a fairy hill, one must walk around it three times widdershins, as Childe Rowland did, calling, 'Open door!' . . . As sacred caves once served as pagan temples, the medieval church forbade their use and claimed that walking or turning one's self widdershins was an indicium of witchcraft."

Witchcraft, of course, was the negative term for many of the ancient goddess religions. But all that's another long story.

In the meantime, it's interesting to see how walking in the direction of the moon becomes "the wrong way." Either/or. Good / bad. How much we have limited our view of the world. No wonder we don't see fairies anymore.

■3■

Arguments with Myself

■ ■ ■ ■ ■

Lilacs in May: A Tribute to Al Purdy

A number of years ago I read an interview with a poet whom I admire, the American Philip Levine, in which he talked about his understanding of literary tradition and what it means to a young writer. One section of that interview has stayed with me ever since and I'd like to quote it now as a way of introducing what I want to say about Al Purdy and his importance to me as a poet. Levine is talking about his love of Keats and he says:

> The Keats . . . that I loved was the Keats of the letters, not the poems, as much as I admire the odes. Because I think that he inherited a poetic tradition that was so puny that he could say, I would jump down Etna for any public good but I want to write beautiful poems. As though you couldn't perform a public good with poetry. And I think you can . . . I mean, you think of all the misery that he saw and you read about it in his letters and how little of it ever gets into his poetry . . . He sits there for months while his brother Tom dies day by day of tuberculosis in what must have been one of the most polluted shitholes in the world, the London of the nineteenth century. And what does he get: 'Here where youth grows pale, and spectre-thin and dies.' Tom gets two lines. And that's it. Bingo. I mean, I couldn't let America take my brother and kill him at seventeen or eighteen, and just sit there and say, 'Well, I have to write poems about Grecian urns.' Shit. I mean I don't think I'd ever get over it. And I don't think Keats wanted to get over it. I don't think that he inherited as strong a tradition as I did. He didn't have Whitman.

What I like about Levine's comments here is the recognition that a literary tradition involves the building of a space in which there is room, safety, *permission*, if you will, to say what you need to say. It's an understanding of tradition that sometimes gets forgotten, since younger writers often tend to think of what has been done before only as a limitation, something we have to escape from, break with, whatever. Both meanings exist, of course, but what I want to talk about here is what it has meant to me, as a writer in this country, to have had Al Purdy as part of my tradition. I want to talk about what I have been allowed to do that I don't believe I could have done without him.

I didn't discover Al Purdy until the early 1970s. One of the main reasons for this was that I was studying English at a university where Canadian Literature had not yet been heard of, let alone been considered fit to scoff at. In fact, I didn't read a Purdy poem until I dropped out of my Ph.D. program. I now believe that the one act was a necessary pre-requisite to the other — and to my becoming a writer, period.

I dropped out of my Ph.D. program angrily, noisily, with outrageous acts and brave words. At the time, all I was able to articulate clearly was that there was too great a gap between what I was studying and what was happening around me. I had been heavily involved in New Left politics since 1963 and by 1969-70 I could no longer handle the tensions and contradictions that existed between what I was living and what I was reading.

That's what I saw then. What I realize now is that underneath that tension were others, less easy to articulate, but much more painful — and much more important to me as a writer. One, of course, was the gender gap, already yawning at this point, between my increasingly radical feminist views and the fact that there were almost no women's voices, anywhere, in the classroom or the literature — and that trying to talk about that (as I did) was quite quickly and very cruelly suppressed. To heal that wound, I would need women writers — and I've found them. But that's another story.

There were other wounds, too. For one, my university education was daily taking me further and further away from my parents, who had worked like hell for me to get it. Not only was it allowing me opportunities they never had, it was teaching me contempt for their lives and for my own class background, my own cultural context. What this meant for me as a writer, I see now, was that I was taught to deny and reject the very stuff, the only stuff, that could give my work as a writer authenticity. I was being robbed of my language and I almost didn't know it. What I felt at the time was simply that I didn't belong in university. I "wasn't good enough."

Or, to put it another way, I was being taught that what I had to say — the only thing I had to say — wasn't "worth saying." That attitude was all around me. In the literature I read, in the classrooms where I studied, people spoke, literally, with the accents of another culture, another class. They made fun of people who said "eh," and who used the flat, everyday speech of rural and working-class southern Ontario. People like my parents, in other words, and my grandparents and my great-grandparents and . . .

Then there were the stories, *what* got said in those carefully-modulated upper-class or pseudo-Oxonian accents. Wonderful stories, certainly, but always, to my ear, happening to someone else, in some other world. And yet the stories I knew — about holding onto the farm, or raising eight kids, or working double shifts, or simply "getting by" (that most profound, as I see now, understatement) — were put down, if they came up at all, as maudlin, sentimental clichés.

And the landscape! My family had lived around Kingston for two hundred years. I knew the countryside as well as I knew my own name. Could not, in fact, separate one from the other. Everything I saw, I saw through their eyes and their work and their love. The only thing was, I didn't know it. And so when I came to study English, I accepted without question that I was going to live in another country now. A country where the grass was greener, the hills softer. A country where words like "moor" and "glen" seemed to fit. A country where the lilacs bloomed in April, not in May — and without any apparent scent.

To put it simply, I gained a great deal from my education, yes. But I lost, too. I lost my family, my history, my language — as well as the smells and shapes and colors of my life. Without those, I could not be the writer I wanted to be.

So I quit school. Not because I understood everything I have just told you, but because I couldn't bear the pain anymore, though I didn't know its cause. I quit and I traveled around Canada, working at various jobs, finally settling in Windsor where I got heavily involved in labor politics, first of all, then in feminist organizations. But while I was traveling, I began to write poetry, most of it bad (and I mean really bad) T.S. Eliot that could have been written by anybody. Even I could tell it was bad. I began to think I'd never write. I really didn't have anything to say. Or rather, nothing I had to say was "worth saying." As you can see, some of my education had been very successful.

What I couldn't see at that point was, of course, *how* to say it.

And that's where Al Purdy comes in. It's 1970, maybe 1971, and I'm standing in a bookstore with a copy of *The Cariboo Horses* in my hand. I have just read "The Country North of Belleville" and "Percy Lawson" and a few others. I am crying like an idiot, right there in the store, getting the book all wet, so that I have to buy it (though I would have anyway, Al). Maudlin, of course. Sentimental as hell. I can hear my old English profs sniffing as they read this.

But I don't really give a shit. At that moment, I arrived, in my own country, with land I recognized under my feet, and people knew around me, and a language I could get my tongue around filling my mouth. Purdy became an important guide for me. After a while, the whole damn world smelled of lilacs. In *May*, too, the way I knew it should.

So, that's what I owe to Purdy in a literary sense. His work gave me permission to write about the people I knew, and the landscape I saw, and — most importantly — in the voice I'd heard in my head all my life. The voice of the men and women in my family. A voice that tells its stories in the same meandering and magical way that highways move through southeastern Ontario, until you understand that what happens in the story, like the landscape around you, is a metaphor for an inner journey, a journey that takes you to the center of the speaker's life, to his or her discoveries about that life and to the mystery that lies there, always. I've taken that voice and that journey and made it my own, of course, but I needed Al Purdy.

That's the Literary Tradition part of my tribute. Now, a story which Al, I'm sure, will try to convince you is apocryphal. I swear it really happened. Only you can decide if it's true.

We're in Kingston, in the late 1970s or early 1980s, and Purdy is giving a reading. I'm there, of course, and one of the things I love about his reading is the way I can't always tell when his introductions leave off and his poems begin. I love how his voice can do that.

Anyway, Al reads his usual stuff, then he starts reading from unpublished material. And in the middle of one he pauses, looks horrified, rips the thing out of the file folder and says, "Jesus Christ that's a terrible poem. I can't read that shit!" There's a stunned silence as he crumples it up, throws it on the floor and goes on to something he can read.

There's a wonderful freedom in that act, for me. A crazy mix of humility and pride, of taking one's work seriously and oneself less so, that I love and admire. Another kind of permission granted — to make mistakes, and say so. To rip it up and get on with it.

So, that's what I owe to Al Purdy. That kind of courage and freedom. But it doesn't seem to be enough just to say so. I'd like to end by reading a poem of mine, one that owes a great deal to Al and the tradition of which he is a part:

INTO THE MIDST OF IT

You'll take a map, of course, and keep it
open in front of you on the dashboard,
though it won't help. Oh, it'll give mileages,
boundary lines, names, that sort of thing,
but there are places yet
where names are powerless
and what you are entering

is like the silence words get lost in
after they've been spoken.

It's the same with the highways.
The terse, comforting numbers
and the signs that anyone can read.
They won't be any good to you now.
And it's not that kind of confidence
you're after anyway.

What you're looking for are the narrower,
unpaved roads that have become
the country they travel over, dreamlike
as the spare farms you catch
in the corner of your eye,
only to lose them
when you turn your head. The curves
that happen without warning
like a change of heart,
as if, after all these journeys,
the road were still feeling
its way through.

A man comes up on your right — blue shirt
patched from the sky — solid and
unsurprised. He doesn't turn his head
at your passing and by the time your eyes move
to the rear-view mirror, the road has changed.
But it's then you begin to notice
other people: women hanging clothes from grey
porches, a clutter of children on the steps.
Like the man, they do not move
as you go by and you try to imagine
how you must look to them: metallic glimmer

on the bright rim of their sky,
disturbing the dust
that settles behind you, slowly,
through the day's heat,
while in your mind's eye, their faces
form and change with the rippling patterns
sun and cloud make on the fields,
like the figures that swim below your thoughts
in the hour between dream and waking.

It makes you think of the people you love,
how their faces look when they don't know you're
　watching them,
so that what you see there
forces you to recognize
how useless your love is, how little
all your hopes, your good intentions
can ever do for them.

Only now, this doesn't hurt any more,
becomes part of your love, in a way,
just as the dry-weather drone of the cicada
belongs to the heat, to the dust that sifts
like ash over the shiny leaves,
this country you're travelling through,
where the farmlands draw their nourishment
from an ancient mountain range,
and houses rise, insistent
as the rock and almost as indifferent,
making all your questions
about why people came here,
what they liked about it,
why they stayed
as meaningless as questions you might ask
of the trees or the earth itself.

You, who have lived your whole life believing
if you made enough plans
you wouldn't need to be afraid,
driving through a countryside
only the road seems to care about,
to rediscover every time it enters
with that kind of love that's partly tenderness
and partly a sort of confidence
you can't put words around.
Like the look
the people at home will give you
when you get there: nonchalant and almost too deep
for you to see, as they turn back
to whatever held them
before you came.

I couldn't have written that without you, Al. Thanks.

■ ■ ■ ■ ■

Why I Don't (Always) Write Short Stories

Two years ago, I wouldn't have had to put the "always" in there. Two
years ago, I thought I would never — indeed, could never — write a
short story, so when I was asked to give a talk on my craft, as part of
my duties as an instructor at the Upper Canada Writers' Workshop in
Kingston, it seemed obvious what I would talk about. I would talk
about why I didn't write short stories and why, just because I'm a narrative poet, people are always asking me why I don't write short stories
and how I thought narrative poetry (at least, the narrative poetry that
I was trying to write) was not (as some people seem to think) a failed

short story, a short story in disguise, an excuse for a short story or anything, really, like a short story except in the way that it used stories to
tell something else.

That is, in fact, what I *did* talk about, in July 1986, when I gave
my talk at the Upper Canada Writers' Workshop. The tape which was
made at the time was intended to be the basis of an essay such as this.
And I thought at the time that it would be a simple matter of trans-
posing my speech to paper, handing it in for publication and collect-
ing the check.

I should have known better, of course. I should have known that
I am an accomplished procrastinator. I should have remembered that I
hate hearing myself on tape. I should have learned (by now, you would
think) that I write from what I am given, not from what I decide. And
I should have recalled (as I manage to in other situations) those lines
of Brecht's about "while you are living / never say never / things will
not stay as they are / and never becomes before the day is out."

So . . . . here I am two years later. I've just listened to the tape,
surprised, as always, to realize that the woman speaking on it is, in fact,
myself and gratified, as always, to learn that, although the voice is
completely unrecognizable, the words are not entirely those of an inar-
ticulate idiot. I actually learned a great deal about narrative poetry that
I didn't know I knew.

And that I still believe. That's important. At the time I gave that
talk, I had just completed *The Stubborn Particulars of Grace*. I was
thinking poetry. Narrative poetry. I figured I was definitely on to something and that something was definitely not short stories.

I had no idea that, a few weeks later . . . but that's another story
and I'll get back to it.

What happened, however, is only a very small part of it. The wider
question of how "what happens" functions in narrative poetry is what
interests me.

To begin at the beginning, then, with a poem:

APPEAL

That family joke every Sunday,
all of us for dinner at Grandma's
and my dad asked to give thanks
always mumbling into his plate
and my grandmother always looking up
to say "I didn't hear half of that,"
and my dad always replying "Well, Mother,
I wasn't just talking to you."
The laugh that followed
so predictable, so necessary
that the whole thing sang in my mind,
joined the steaming bowls and platters
moving hand to hand above my head
with the slow, clean words
my aunts and uncles used
to make an anecdote or a bit of gossip
into the story of their lives, that world
I found mysterious as their names became
when I looked at their faces or their arms.

When I look at my mother
on a night in 1953, or maybe '55,
sitting on the lawn at the cottage
with my dad and Frank and Helen, the Americans
from across the lake, who've come over
with a bottle of gin and some Marlboros,
which my father is enjoying, though my mother,
her posture what Protestantism becomes
when the protest's gone, sits prim and uncomfortable.
I'm inside, trying to sleep,
but you can tell it's too hot by how the sheet's
already clinging to my legs, itching

like the bites on my arms, the whine
of another mosquito in here somewhere,
the air so close my mother's voice
comes right in — "OK, Frank, give me
one of those things; maybe the smoke'll
keep those bugs away!" — bringing my head
up to the window sill, to her face
laughing in the match flare, tip
of the cigarette that lights my father's
face and Frank's and Helen's too
glints off glass and the metal
rim of lawn chairs. Even the lake
stops nudging the dock for a minute,
lets the night come in, as it can
maybe once, twice, in the whole summer,
when the dark fills up that hot, still air
with something close to clarity.

But what can I call that glimpse
I had then? Or explain why it shines
from my mother still, sets off
what I love in her? How the look
on my father's face (that look,
I see now, that happens when those we love
reveal, as they did the first time,
something we thought we'd lost
to the work of simply getting by)
burns through my memory, lights up
whatever I know of their marriage, of the weariness
and caring and surprise that brought me here
and from which I watch my own kid
take his bearings from some act of mine,
caught briefly, at a distance
further than that night seems now.

A night I offer you, those faces
cupped by darkness, lake and shoreline
as a hand cups a match for the moment
it is needed, even in a light wind,
unable to tell you more or why.
Caught, as I used to be
by that trick an aunt or uncle'd use
of always stopping right at the best part
to take a bite of pie, a sip of tea,
their way of leaning back to look
around the table, let the story sink right in.
As if they hoped to find
that opening in each of us
from which, long after we'd been told
what happened next, they could begin
their slower, more miraculous
returns.

All my life, I have been listening to stories. That Sunday pilgrimage to my Grandmother's, the dinner with the family, the stories — all that "really happened" to me as a small child, in Harrowsmith, Ontario where my grandparents lived after leaving the farm a mile and a half up the highway. But what I remember of that time is not the stories themselves, but the way in which they were told. I remember laughter, response, contradiction, argument, more laughter — all of which seemed incomprehensible at the time. And when I try to write about it, it is that "incomprehensibility" which I am trying to explore, which I enter, as soon as the poem "takes off."

Incomprehensibility is a big and awkward word. Riddle, then. Mystery, if you will. I can't *explain* it any better than that, though in a poem like "Appeal" some of it could be explained by saying that the speaker is remembering herself as a young girl, trying to puzzle out the codes and rituals of adult society. But that is not all it is, or was, even then, for me.

Not long ago, I happened upon an essay by John Berger which put into words some of what I'm getting at. Berger may be best known as an art-critic for his book *Ways of Seeing*, though he is also the author of several other such studies, as well as novels, short essays, and the film-script for the film *Joshua, Who Will be Twenty-Five in the Year 2000*. For the last several years, Berger has lived in a small peasant village in the south of France, a situation which has greatly affected his critical and other writing. The essay I am referring to now — "The Storyteller" in *The Sense of Sight* — is about the tradition of story-telling in peasant communities. In it, Berger talks about how the stories function within the community, both in the way they record what happens in the village and in the way in which they testify to what that *means*:

> Sometimes there is a moral judgment implicit in the story, but this judgment — whether just or unjust —remains a detail: the story *as a whole* is told with some tolerance because it involves those with whom the storyteller and listener are going to go on living.
> Very few stories are narrated either to idealize or condemn; rather, they testify to the always slightly surprising range of the possible.

Now, I know that a remote peasant village in the south of France is quite a ways from the family of a dairy farmer, eating Sunday dinner in Harrowsmith, Ontario, but I recognize what Berger is describing. Especially when he says:

> The story invites comment. Indeed it creates it, for even total silence is taken as a comment. The comments maybe spiteful or bigoted, but, if so, they themselves will become a story and thus, in turn, become subject to comment . . . More usually, the comments, which add to the story, are intended and taken as the commentator's personal response — in the light of that story — to the riddle of existence. Each story allows everyone to define himself.

Or herself. One of the other things I remember from those Sundays are the stories that were not told at the dinner table, but in the kitchen by my grandmother and her daughters and daughters-in-law, as they prepared food or did the dishes. Even as a child, I recognized that these stories were different. For one thing, they were exclusively about women. Women's lives and women's bodies. Men, if they figured at all, did so from the perimeter of the story, or as the object of ridicule and — though, rarely — undisguised anger.

The stories moved differently, too. Around *things* and tasks. Was the turkey done? Do you think I should add more salt to these peas? Could you go out to the garden and get some tomatoes, ripe ones now, pay attention to what you're picking. The story's ability to move through *and use* these diversions was itself a testimony to the power of the teller as well as that of the listener. It is a power I witness, still, among women talking together — whether over coffee, with children running around or at a meeting where *how* an issue is decided is as important as the issue itself.

The atmosphere of those kitchens was always, as I remember it, electric. A sense of subversion was clearly palpable. And this had to do, not only with the events of the story, but with how the telling moved through it, picking up the diversions and interruptions, comments and digressions, as it went along. *That* is what I hear when I am writing my poems. And that is how I try to write them.

I do not mean to imply, however, that none of this happened at the dinner table. I am familiar with — and find useful — current language theory which talks about "dominant discourse" and women's silence. And that happened, of course, in my family as elsewhere. But it was not *all* that happened and current language theory, like any other theory, cannot explain all that we have to tell about ourselves. At the dinner table, my grandmother, my aunts, and my mother certainly did their share of the talking. What was talked about here, however, was their shared life. If the perspective in the kitchen was one of gender, that of the dinner table was one of class.

Class and community. One could not — or at least my grandmother could not — tell a story about anyone in the village or in her past without embarking on what I call the Classical Genealogical Digression. You know what I mean, I'm sure. X is introduced as the main character of the story, but introducing X means mentioning that he or she is the daughter of Y who married one of the B's from C, whose sister — the one with the crippled hand, what was her name? — ran off with the bootlegger and . . . you know what I mean. You also recognize, by this time I hope, that that too is part of the story.

Or there's the Past History Digression, in which a story about K cannot be complete without remembering the time he got into that fight in the churchyard with the minister's son or how his youngest child drowned, seventeen years ago, on a picnic. What is to be told about him now — and what that even means in terms of the Whole Story — can only be understood (you understand) in the light of these other events just as they can only be understood in the light of . . .

Get it?

That's how I try to get my poem to move. That's what I want you to hear — and encounter — in your own life.

If the peripheral figures in the women's stories were men, those of the dinner-table stories were city folk, bosses, supervisors. There was the same tone of ridicule and mocking disbelief. There was, around the table, a similar atmosphere of power and subversion. And again, it was an atmosphere I would enter as a young adult when I became involved in the politics of the sixties. It was a tone I would hear in the stories of civil rights workers and draft-dodgers. I would hear it, too, when I began to work with others on an oral history of the founding of the UAW in Canada, in the voices of old men — and some women — who knew that while Official History has little, if anything, to say about them, that does not make them silent or powerless. They know what they know and here are the stories as testimony.

So. That's what I try to make happen in my poems. I don't think of it consciously. But I hear it. For me, writing a poem is a journey of discovering — no, not discovering, getting closer to — the "riddle of existence." And for me, the narrative elements of the poem, the stories, "what happened," are part of an extended metaphor for that journey. But the poem as a whole is the voice, discovering.

> Poems, even when narrative, do not resemble stories. All stories are about battles, of one kind or another, which end in victory and defeat. Everything moves towards the end, when the outcome will be known.
>
> Poems, regardless of any outcome, cross the battlefields, tending the wounded, listening to the wild monologues of the triumphant or the fearful. They bring a kind of peace. Not by anaesthesia or easy reassurance, but by recognition and the promise that what has been experienced cannot disappear as if it had never been. Yet the promise is not of a monument. (Who, still on a battlefield, wants monuments?) The promise is that language has acknowledged, has given shelter, to the experience which demanded, which cried out.
>
> Poems are nearer to prayers than to stories, but in poetry there is no one behind the language being prayed to. It is the language itself which has to hear and acknowledge.

Berger, again. I'm not nuts about the battle analogy for stories. I'm not sure it's entirely accurate (though when I think about it, most of the stories I heard — still hear — are about victory and defeat). Anyway. I like what he says about poetry. I believe it. I try to write from it.

Which means, too, that the voice of the narrative poem — as I hear and try to write it — is somewhat collective. I say *somewhat* collective, because I recognize that it is also private, specific to a particular person in a particular place, at a particular time. I say *collective* because I want to convey that it is most emphatically not "universal," in the sense of Universal Human Experience. Such experience does not really exist; what our culture often refers to as such has historically been white, male, and upper-class. But we do have a collective experience — collective as in choir or political movement — in which the whole grows from, but does not transcend, its separate parts.

This narrative voice is, I think, much different from the lyrical voice, which I hear as a testimony to what is unique and private and sometimes lonely in us. That voice, with its power for taking the reader on an inner journey, is a necessary part of what we are. In fact, it would be interesting, in another essay, to explore the relationship between the power and presence of the lyric voice and our understanding of ourselves at this point in history. For me it would involve, as well, asking why the presence of the narrative voice is less in evidence and why people are always asking me why I don't write short stories instead.

Which brings us full circle. I am, now, writing short stories, but not because I think they are the same as, or even the next logical step after, narrative poems. I am writing short stories right now because that's what I have been given to write.

Or rather, that's what I've chosen to do with what I've been given. These women just started talking in my head; I chose to listen and to see where it would take me. I don't know enough about the process yet to explore it in the way that I have tried to explore my poetry. I suspect that it has something to do with what Flannery O'Connor calls "the mystery of personality." In a good story we encounter that mystery in a specific person, in a specific situation, at a specific time. In that sense, it has connections with my narrative poetry. But how we approach that mystery seems, to me at least, altogether different.

"How different" I can only explain by gesturing again towards what Berger says about the sense of immediate testimony, of prayer, which is inherent in poetry. Immediate acknowledgement. I know that, for me, only poetry allows this to happen. Prose allows for something else, which I am only beginning to understand. Ideally, I want to continue exploring both.

I write from what I am given. Not just images, words, sounds, voices. But a particular life, as a woman, in a particular family and community, at this time in history. I can explain how I write — and in this essay I have tried to explain — by telling you some of the story of my life. But I can't explain all of it. I do not believe that any story or any theory can. There is always that mystery — that "slightly surprising range of the possible" — to which I can simply gesture. Testify. And that, for me as a writer — and as a reader — is, for now at least, enough.

■ ■ ■ ■ ■

English Literature: It's Still a Man's World

Last night, I spent some time going over the books my son will read this semester in his Grade 9 English course. It was good to see my old favorites. They still read *Julius Caesar,* and the poetry anthology includes Browning's "How They Brought the Good News from Ghent to Aix" and Frost's "Stopping By Woods On a Snowy Evening," two poems whose words and rhythms I can still recall, perfectly, after over 30 years.

Good stuff, this. I think that my son will enjoy reading it as much as I did. He's enthusiastic, he has an excellent teacher. The books, which also include a selection of various mythologies and another of shorter plays, will give him a good introduction to English literature.

It will not give him a well-rounded one. For the most part, the work he will read has been written by men. Out of 80-odd poems by some 50 authors, only one is written by a woman. The short-play anthology contains nine selections; one is by a woman and another is based on a story written by a woman. In addition, most of the characters (save for Caesar's wife and the goddesses in the myths) will be men.

If men and women in our culture had the same experiences, then the gender of the authors whose books our children read would be irrelevant. In the best of all possible worlds, we could talk about *human* experience and mean just that.

In this world, however, we can't. What my son will be reading this semester is *male* human experience, presented as if it represents the whole. Too bad for him. Worse yet for his female classmates.

I'd like to explore some of the reasons for this situation. Let's start with Shakespeare. I know that there were few, if any, female play-wrights in the 16th century. What I'd like my son to learn is why.

One way to do this might be to give students an excerpt from Virginia Woolf's famous essay on women and writing, "A Room Of One's Own." In the part I'm thinking of, Woolf admits that "it would have been impossible, completely and entirely, for any woman to have written the plays of Shakespeare in the age of Shakespeare." But then she goes on to explore why: "Let me imagine, since facts are so hard to come by, what would have happened had Shakespeare had a wonder-fully gifted sister, called Judith, let us say."

Woolf then paints Judith's life — how she was not sent to school, though her brother Will was. How she was set to household tasks whenever she tried to learn to read. She follows Shakespeare's own life — running off to London, beginning his career by holding horses at the stage door and then getting work in the theater. What would have happened to Judith had she tried this? Woolf imagines her alone in London, with no education and no training. An actor takes pity on her and before long, she finds herself pregnant with his child. In Woolf's story, she kills herself, for "who can imagine the heat and vio-lence of the poet's heart when caught and tangled in a woman's body?"

I think this excerpt from Woolf would spark some lively discus-sion in a Grade 9 class, raise some valuable questions. Side by side with Shakespeare's play, it would encourage students to think hard about human experience, male and female.

We could also include some diaries and letters from the period, many of which were written by women.

Or there's Lady Winchilsea, also mentioned by Woolf, writing in 1661:

Alas! a woman that attempts the pen,
Such a presumptuous creature is esteemed.
The fault can by no virtue be redeemed.
They tell us we mistake our sex and way;
Good breeding, fashion, dancing, dressing play,
Are the accomplishments we should desire.

"But it's all so angry," you say, "it's all so depressing." True. So are large parts of *Julius Caesar*. "And it's all negative," someone else complains, "you make the actor out to be a rapist and the poem seems to blame men for not letting women write. It makes men look bad."

Yes, perhaps it does. On the other hand, we don't object to our children reading about Lady Macbeth. And does it make men look bad, or does it simply question the values we live by? As Woolf points out in another essay:

"It is probable, however, that both in life and in art the values of a woman are not the values of a man. Thus, when a woman comes to write a novel, she will find that she is perpetually wishing to alter the established values — to make serious what appears insignificant to a man, and trivial what is to him important. And for that, of course, she will be criticized . . ."

Criticized and not published. In my son's anthology, for example, we have Robert Browning. Why not Elizabeth? We have Edgar Allen Poe; why not Emily Dickinson? We have F. R. Scott and Earle Birney; why not P.K. Page and Dorothy Livesay? Since most school budgets require that they use anthologies, rather than separate works of the sort I suggested, this question is important. Why is women's writing consistently excluded?

The 50% Solution, a study compiled by Anne Innis Dagg, attempts to answer this question. It is full of useful statistics which indicate that the amount of women's writing found in anthologies and little magazines or published in book form is disproportionate to the number of women writing. Women writers account for over half the membership in organizations like The Writers' Union of Canada. Yet

out of 14 anthologies of Canadian literature (poetry and prose) published since 1980 only five contain 50 per cent or more women's work.
As well, fewer books by women than by men are published and
women receive fewer reviews of their work in mainstream papers and
magazines. Women also receive a much smaller chunk of the grants
available to artists through organizations such as The Canada Council.

While none of this exclusion bears any relation to the number of
women actually writing, it does seem to be affected by whether or not
the editor of an anthology is male or female, by the proportion of
women to men on arts council juries and by the number of women
reviewers. When women have some say, women's writing gets recognized. When men get to decide, it doesn't.

"Ah, but is the work submitted by women as good as the work
submitted by men?" I hear you ask. A fair question, since I am not sug-
gesting that work of inferior quality be published just to right the balance. But the real question is, surely, who decides? And by what
standards? As Virginia Woolf indicated, men seem unable to appreciate work written by women. But does that mean it is inferior?

Of course not. Women write as we do because of our experience
in the world and our experience in the world is different from that of
men. Yet we are judged, not by how well we write, but by how closely
our view of the world approximates theirs. As a result, women's writing
is deemed inferior rather than simply different. Or, as Woolf put it,
"weak or trivial or sentimental."

And so, my son will read little by women this year. This absence
will teach him a great deal. It will teach him that human experience
is the same as male experience. Therefore, he doesn't need to question
how he sees things. It will teach him that the experience of women is
not something he can learn from. Therefore, he doesn't need to listen
when women speak or believe what he hears us say.

You think I'm exaggerating? Read the newspapers. Every day
women are disbelieved when we try to tell our stories; crimes committed against us are repeatedly trivialized by the light sentences given to
those who commit them. Women who speak strongly and positively
about women are seen as angry, shrill man-haters.

My son — and his female classmates — will learn all this just by living in the world. I'd like to think their schooling gave them the opportunity to learn something else, something they could use to become fuller human beings. I'd like to think that's what the study of literature was all about. Why can't it be?

■ ■ ■ ■ ■

Teaching Kids the Power and Grace of Poetry

There's this story going around that kids these days can't read and write. They couldn't parse a sentence if their Walkmans depended on it. They haven't looked up from the TV long enough to read anything, even the writing on the side of the cereal box at breakfast, since they were born.

That story is frequently accompanied by another one. This one is about how the language is being destroyed by words that aren't really words and spellings that are incorrect and grammatical usages that aren't according to Fowler (or some other, equally fusty, authority). Both stories end with a moral: none of this would happen if we all got back to the basics.

As a writer, I have a problem with these stories. If people aren't reading any more, how come book sales in the country — especially of our literature — are so high? If our language is being destroyed, how come there's an increasing interest in poetry in Canada? And I don't mean just reading poetry. I mean writing it.

As any bleary-eyed editor of any literary magazine in this country can tell you, there is lots of poetry being written and submitted these days. And a lot of it is very, very good. But the new poetry that I'm most familiar with is being written by kids. Good poetry, too. Lots of it, written by those very people who aren't supposed to be able to read or to know a verb from a participle, dangling or otherwise.

In fact, the interest in poetry among schoolchildren is so great that one school board — the Peterborough County Board of Education — has chosen to devote four days and several thousand dollars to the Peterborough Poetry Festival. I've just come back from this festival and I'm exhausted. It's that good kind of exhaustion, though, the kind that comes from working with people whose energy and excitement is so great that sleep becomes unimportant.

The people I was working with were school children from Grades 7 through 13, from both separate and public schools in the Peterborough area. One hundred and sixty potential poets whose talent and enthusiasm kept the thirteen professional poets, who'd been brought in to lead the workshops, going nonstop.

Workshops, workshops, workshops. We had workshops on Imagist poetry, on metaphor, or haiku and dramatic monologue and rhyme. Workshops on editing and publishing, love poetry, autobiographical poetry. We pretended we were vegetables; we explored landscapes familiar and foreign, real and imagined. We made poems out of sounds and gestures, poems that incorporated pictures and photographs.

One group worked for two days to incorporate all their individual poems into a performance piece. On the final day of the festival, everyone gathered in the common room for the performance. I was touched by the power and sophistication of the performance itself, and by the way in which it was received by the audience. There was very little of the giggling and shuffling and talking that we usually associate with gatherings of this sort. Everyone — and I mean everyone — was paying attention. Not the sort of attention that is paid because Mr. So-and-so is watching and you'll get a detention if you don't shut up, but real attention, from the heart, to something that mattered.

And it was that sort of attention that I felt all week, a sense of absolute engagement, of a concentration so intense that people forgot to take breaks, and grumbled when the two-hour sessions were over.

Engagement with what? With the self, first of all, with all the shifting, uncertain, joyful, crazy, painful, and powerful elements that make up what we are. Writing poetry involves that state which the poet John Keats described as "negative capability," that "being in uncertainties, mysteries, doubts, without any irritable reaching after fact and reason." The workshops explored ways to express these different selves; people adopted the identities of various animals, for example, and spoke through their voices. Or they wrote legends of themselves, using figures from myth and fairytale to express their own real feelings.

Engagement, with the forbidden, too, all those parts of the self that we do not always allow to speak or are punished for expressing or don't know how to. Everything that poetry allows because it is rooted in the unconscious and, as Adrienne Rich puts it, "presses too close against the barriers of repression." Too close, sometimes, to be "sayable" in the conventional way, using the usual rules of grammar. Some workshops explored other ways of speaking, using sound and gesture, for example, or paying close attention to how the words can be placed on the page — where you break a line, how you punctuate it — to express what you want to say. This is the power that poetry has always had. The power to push against the limits of language.

Engagement with language, then. For, ultimately, that is what the writing of poetry — and these workshops — is about. How do you write a poem that describes the flight of geese? How do you construct a sentence that makes the reader *feel* as well as see their flight? What sort of sentence could it be? What sort of words would you use to describe the geese you see? What happens to your flock if you compare it to a "snowplowing skier" as Galway Kinnell does in a poem? What if you compare it to an airplane? How does that change what sort of geese they are?

These are questions that I asked a group of teenagers in one of my workshops. The discussion of their answers involved discussion of grammar, syntax, imagery, metaphor, and modern poetry. It involved the teaching of language as a *living* language, something that changes and can be changed to fit what needs to be said. The discussion involved as well the recognition that there were no "right" answers, that each of us was looking for the word or the sentence or the sound best suited to the poem we were writing — and no other.

"You cannot learn by watching," says Canadian magician Doug Henning, "you can only learn by doing." This is true, I believe, for becoming a magician, a carpenter, a windsurfer, a parent — or a poet. We can talk all we want about teaching the "basics" (as if they were always the same, in every time and context), about getting our children to read, about being grammatically correct, but until they are engaged with language where it matters — where language becomes the means by which they say what they want to say — the language they learn is not their own.

The Peterborough Poetry Festival cost about $15,000. Half of that was paid by the Board; the League of Canadian Poets picked up the rest. The League's money comes from the Ontario Arts Council, which funds a province-wide program called Poets in the Schools. Any school in Ontario can get financial assistance to bring poets into the classroom for readings and workshops. Similar funding is also available for prose writers, through The Writers' Union of Canada.

But besides being willing to spend the money, the Peterborough Board is willing to spend the time. The teachers involved in the festival put in a lot of hours planning this event, which is unique in Canada. Even at the end of four days of administrative craziness, those involved were already talking of doing it next year.

Creative writing is now part of the English curriculum in most schools in Ontario. In the 10 years that I have been going into schools to give readings and to teach workshops, I have seen an improvement in language skills and in the ability to read and appreciate poetry. I believe that this has a lot to do with the attention being paid to creative writing.

Another benefit of the Peterborough Poetry Festival is that it brings student poets together with each other and with a wide variety of professional poets. It says that being a writer is as possible as becoming an engineer.

Something like this happens in Kingston, Ontario during the

Young Authors Conferences, organized for both elementary and high school students, at various times during the year. But we could use more. I'd like to see a Kingston Poetry Festival. As a writer, I think it's vital — if we're serious about teaching our children a love for and a grace with language. As a taxpayer, I can't think of a better way to spend $15,000.

Last word to one of our young poets. These lines are from a poem describing spring, but like all good poems, it opens up other meanings as well. I like to read it as a poem about writing, too:

Under my white feet,
I feel the grass growing,
and each blade pushes me taller.

— Julie Treadwell

■　■　■　■　■

Shyly Slipping a Poem from the Purse

Okay out there, get ready. This is another piece about poetry. I can't help it. July is poetry month for me. I've been teaching at the Upper Canada Writers' Workshop in Kingston, Ontario for two weeks and now at the Summer School of the Arts for St. Lawrence College in Brockville. I think poetry and eat it and dream it and if I have a few minutes to weed my garden, I tell my plants about it too. I don't know if it's the poems or the mulch, but my cucumbers are doing fine.

Anyway, poetry. Most people I know think they hate it or that they don't understand it or that poetry is only written (and understood) by strange beings who sit around drinking black coffee and staring moodily at the moon.

At the same time — and this to me is stranger and more wonderful than the most obscure poem ever written — most people I
know have written at least one poem in their lives. I mean, everybody.
Supermarket checkout clerks and kindergarten kids and plumbers and
taxi drivers and housewives and prison guards and police officers and
nurses and babies. Everywhere I go, as soon as people ask me what I do
for a living and I say "write poetry," I know what will happen next. A
shy smile, first. Then a little giggle or a cough. Then, very softly, "Well
I wrote a poem once too. Do you think you could read it?" And out of
the pocket or the purse or the school scribbler or the memory will
come a poem.

So what am I to make of all this? What do I make of the fact that
every year, all over this country, all sorts of unlikely people, from stock-
brokers to strippers, come out of the closet for a week or so at some
workshop somewhere and reveal themselves as (blush, stammer) poets.
The very same people — and you must understand this to understand
how truly amazing this situation is — the very same people who might,
in other situations say that they didn't understand poetry at all.

It would seem that we are a nation of poets too shy to admit it.

Let's get back to the bit about not understanding poetry, though.
Why do we imagine that we don't? My own feeling is that some of
this happens because of the way poetry is taught, when it is taught, in
schools. There's a strong tendency to treat poetry as a problem that
has to be solved, about something no ordinary mortal could understand, rather than as a communication from one human being to
another, full of feelings and hopes and wishes and dreams that everyone shares, one way or another.

What I like about poetry is the economy of its communication,
the way it uses the surprises of an image to say what it takes most of us
paragraphs to say. In a poem called "When You Go Away", for example, W. S. Merwin says everything about the pain of being left and how
hard it is to talk about it in two lines:

My words are the garment of what I shall never be
Like the tucked sleeve of a one-armed boy.

Besides being taught as a problem, the poetry we teach our children in school tends to ignore the fact that real poetry happens everywhere all the time, in every age. I meet hundreds of high-school students every year who say they hate poetry. When I ask them what they've read, they mention the usual classics — Keats, Shakespeare, Milton, etc. All great poets, true, but not the way to start enjoying poetry when you're 15. These same people listen to Talking Heads, David Bowie, Bruce Springsteen, and Kate Bush — all of whom are sophisticated, complex lyricists — with no trouble at all. In reading poetry, it seems to me we should follow the rule we have for writing poetry: Start with what you know, with what you love, and see where it takes you. Anyone who ignores rock and roll as a major 20th century poetic form is ignoring the energy, the surprise, the passion that is the basis of all good poetry in any age.

That's one problem. Another is the idea that poetry has to be about Great Themes without really thinking about what those Great Themes are. In the past, when most poems were written by white, upper-class men, both the content and the style, which were strong in classical references and biblical themes, reflected their world view as if it were *the* world view. The resistance that students have to this poetry is real and legitimate. To continue to teach this poetry as the only good poetry cuts us off from all sorts of other possibilities.

One example of other possibilities is the work of poet Tom Wayman. Wayman has constantly and quite rightly pointed out that one of the themes missing from the classical poetry of the past is that of work. One of the contributions that Wayman has made to Canadian poetry is to collect poems about work from other people. He has published several anthologies of work poetry. The best two are *A Government Job at Last* and *Going for Coffee*. Both contain wonderfully energetic examples of modern poetry written by ordinary people as well as established poets:

"Sometimes I pretend I'm stupid," writes cab-driver David Beaver in a poem called "Love Goes Out of Style," "and satisfied with the life / of a cabbie / After all, I tell myself / where else is there to go / that you haven't been to / at least twice today."

And British Columbia fisherman Kevin Roberts writes: "the fish come in dancing / iridescent / dark torpedoes / flurry of silver / spray / as they jump."

"Some day I'm gonna stand up on my desk / take all my clothes off / and hurl the typewriter at your head," begins a poem by secretary Diedre Gallagher. "Someday, I'm gonna claim compensation / for mind rot / and soul destruction."

In some countries — Nicaragua, for example — poets like Ernesto Cardinale and Chilean poet Pablo Neruda are national heroes. Everyone can recite some of their work. Their pictures appear on the streets and at large rallies. In other countries — Chile, El Salvador, Hungary, Guatemala — poets are imprisoned, sometimes tortured. Both these facts are testimonies to the power of poetry, to the fact that it manages to speak a truth and to demand a response in a way that no other art form can.

In our country we don't jail our poets, but we do silence them in other ways. We tend to say that poetry about work, poetry about women, by people of color, dub poetry (which is poetry that grows out of the language and music of West Indian people in Canada) is not "real" poetry. As a result, we deprive ourselves and our children of a whole world — and of their place in it.

A friend lends me an anthology of literature by women with disabilities, *With Wings*. I open it to a poem called "Diminishment" by Nancy Mairs, a woman whose disability is multiple sclerosis:

> My body
> is going away
> It fades
> to the transparency
> of rubbed amber
> held against the sun.
> It shrinks
> it grows quiet.

Small, quiet
it is a cold
and heavy
smoothed stone.
Who will have it
when it lies
pale and polished
as a clean bone?

What I want to know is why this poem does not appear in the anthologies we use in our high schools. Why can it only be found in an anthology by and about women with disabilities? What does that say about us as a society? What are we afraid of?

The poets themselves are not afraid. Every year I see them by the dozens. Some of them will end up being published poets some day. Many more will never do that, and what's more they don't care. They just want to write the poem for the joy of it, the sheer joy and power of making sense of their lives in words, on paper. Getting it down. Getting down to it.

The other evening I took some time off from poetry workshops to attend a party at a friend's house near Sydenham. Her four-year-old son Nicholas takes me for a walk. It's just about dark, a beautiful, still evening, the fire-flies are out and Nick has his sword with him just in case we run into dragons, which, as he and I know, are everywhere. Nick is telling me how he has a father and his father has a father, and *his* father has a father and how everyone has a mother too and some people have brothers and step-brothers and sisters and pets.

"It's all connected, you see," he says, taking my hand. "Dogs and frogs and cartoons and candy and fathers and sisters and dragons and everything. Everyone's different and it's all connected."

He pauses to let me take this in.

"And that," he says quietly just as the sun slips, finally, down, "that is why the world is such an exciting place."

See what I mean? Everyone's a poet.

■ ■ ■ ■ ■

Finding Some Unsuspected Truths in Fiction

One of my favorite quotes about writing has always been American writer Jessamyn West's observation that "fiction reveals truths that reality obscures." I think of it as a statement of faith in the power of language, especially in the power of the story, to touch and change us.

I remember when I first read Doris Lessing's *The Golden Notebook*. It was a couple of years after the novel first came out in 1963; I was a university student at the time, with classes to attend and essays to write. But what I did was read that novel — all 600-odd pages of it — in a day and a half, stopping only to grab a sandwich or a glass of milk, mesmerized by the fact that my own thoughts and feelings were suddenly there, larger-than-life-size in the writing of a woman whose upbringing and experience had been very different from mine and who was still able to show me certain aspects of my own life as if she herself had lived it. A woman who was able, moreover, to teach me certain things about my life which I had been unable to learn simply by living it, simply because I was "too close." When I think back to my university days I remember *The Golden Notebook* as one of the most significant books I ever read, though it was not on any of my English courses.

The experience of discovering myself — or parts of myself — in a novel has occurred since then, and always with the same sense of wonder and delight. The luxury of being able to read a novel in a day or so has been less frequent. One of the joys of my time at the University of Western Ontario last fall was the rediscovery of that kind of reading, the opportunity to enter a book as if it were another country and live there with its inhabitants for as long as I wanted. Over the fall, my reading took a new direction, too. And the books that I "lived in" the longest had nothing to do with my own experience at all. I began to live in other lives, lives that could never, ever be mine. And in doing so, I learned, once again and at a deeper level, the truth of Ms. West's observation about the power of fiction.

The first of these is Zora Neale Hurston's *Their Eyes Were Watching God*, a novel originally published in 1937. Ms. Hurston is one of the few female writers to come out of a period in Afro-American literature usually referred to as "The Harlem Renaissance," one of a handful of black writers whose work received some recognition during the early part of this century. Hurston was an important figure — a black nationalist, a tireless recorder of the dialects, customs, and folklore of her people. She was witty, intelligent, beautiful, proud — all reasons to make her often unpopular with "white folks" who considered her too uppity. She died in 1960 in a Florida welfare home, and is buried in an unmarked grave in a segregated cemetery in Fort Pierce, Florida, a grave which Alice Walker describes as "a resting place generally symbolic of the black writer's fate in America."

What is powerful about the novel for me is the language. Listen to how Ms. Hurston describes a group of rural villagers, sitting on their porches at the end of the day: "These sitters had been tongueless, earless, eyeless conveniences all day long. Mules and other brutes had occupied their skins. But now, the sun and the bossman were gone, so the skins felt powerful and human. They became lords of sounds and lesser things. They passed nations through their mouths."

This is a novel about a black woman and her struggle to find freedom not only from racism, but also from sexism. It is the first black novel to break the "Aunt Jemima" stereotype which worked — and still works — as a means of doubly oppressing black women. And its power comes in a large part from the language Ms. Hurston uses, the language she heard every day from the people around her. It took me to worlds I had never imagined, because it evoked voices I had never been allowed to hear.

Then there was Toni Morrison's Pulitzer-Prize-winning novel, *Beloved*. Set in 1873, this novel explores the world of Baby Suggs, Sethe, Denver, Paul D, and others, former slaves who are now, because of the Underground Railway and the Emancipation Proclamation, "free." It is the most powerful, most poetic novel I have read in at least

10 years. It shamed me, reading it, to realize how little I really "knew" about slavery, how little the few facts I had learned had ever translated themselves into real, felt, human experience.

Take this description of Baby Suggs (a 70-year-old slave) on her arrival in Ohio on the Underground Railway: " . . . suddenly she saw her hands and thought with a clarity as simple as it was dazzling, 'These hands belong to me. These are my hands.' Next she felt a knocking in her chest and discovered something else new: her own heartbeat. Had it been there all along? This pounding thing?"

Or this description of Paul D's experience of a chain-gang prison in which the men were kept in ditches "one thousand feet of earth — five feet deep, five feet wide, into which wooden boxes had been fitted." When the men awoke in the morning they could hear the doves singing, but they had "neither the right nor the permission to enjoy it because in that place mist, doves, sunlight, copper dirt, moon — everything belonged to the men who had the guns. [They] could stop you from hearing doves or loving moonlight. So you protected yourself and loved small."

Or Sethe's own realization, a few days after she escapes on the railway, that "freeing yourself was one thing; claiming ownership of that free self was another."

From there I went to Dionne Brand's first collection of short stories, *Sans Souci.* Dionne is a poet whose work I have long admired; she was born in the Caribbean and has lived in Canada for the last 18 years. Her stories grow from the experience of living in two worlds, neither of which feels like "home," the Caribbean because it has been left behind, Canada because people of color do not feel welcome here.

Of the three books, this last was the hardest, I guess, because what was being described was the country I live in, the cities I visit. Yet I was forced to face the fact that the country I live in is a very different country from that of the characters in these stories. In "Train to Montreal," Ms. Brand describes a "simple" trip to the train washroom: "she walked, not looking but feeling the eyes of strangers turning toward her. She disturbed the little vignettes of white people sleeping or reading in their seats. Faces turned quickly toward her and away. Was there annoyance in their looks? . . . Past one cabin, past another from which smoke, beer, white men's voices blasted out. From this one she caught a grimy tableau, a smell of sweat. Eyes lighting up into a leer at her passing. Quickly. Fear, spreading fern-like through her. Maybe they would grab her, kill her, who knows."

The pain in all of these novels is palpable, real as wind or sunshine. But there is power here too — in Ms. Hurston's use of language, especially in her dialogue; in the immediacy of Ms. Morrison's vision of history; in Ms. Brand's imagery and in her politics. In all three novels there is a *celebration* of black women which even the pain cannot diminish. All three novels glow with their power, their intelligence, their determination to survive.

For me, reading these novels was like opening the door — just a crack — on a landscape so vast that I cannot at present imagine its dimensions. I have only begun to explore it. And with that beginning exploration come the usual questions, questions I must ask both of my culture and of myself. Why did it take so long for me to find these books? How long did it take for them to be researched, written, published? Under what difficulties, difficulties that I, as a white writer, do not know? Are they being used, currently, in high schools and universities in this country? If not, why not?

And always, I come back to Zora Neale Hurston, a celebrity in her time. Briefly. Then the welfare home, the unmarked grave. How far have other women of color, especially women writers, come? How much will this culture preserve of Ms. Morrison? Ms. Brand? What can we do to prevent Ms. Hurston's history from repeating itself?

The Contemplative Life: A Necessity as Well as a Limitation for the Writer

I spent last Sunday the way a lot of you probably did — at a barbecue. The food was your regular barbecue food — chicken, salad, rolls, sliced tomatoes, red wine — and there were the usual problems with mosquitoes and soggy paper plates. What made my barbecue different from any of yours, I'll bet, was that it was held in a garden at Peter's Abbey in Muenster, Saskatchewan, and was prepared by Benedictine monks. Most of them were still wearing their cassocks. Except for the one doing the chicken; he had on black clerical pants and a T-shirt that read "#1 Father." The monk who carried out the salads, still in his cassock, was wearing a peaked cap that said, "Jesus was a Carpenter, too."

What, you may ask, was a feminist doing at a Benedictine monastery? Answer: daydreaming, dawdling, doodling — all those things I used to get in trouble for at school.

Most of my life as a writer is spent trying to find the time to write. It's a lot like the struggle described by a character in a story by Alice Munro: "In my own house, I seemed to be often looking for a place to hide — sometimes from the children but more often from the jobs to be done and the phone ringing and the sociability of the neighbors. I wanted to hide so that I could get busy at my real work, which was a sort of wooing of distant parts of myself."

My two weeks of St. Peter's Abbey were the longest period of time I had been away from my usual life as a working mother since my son was born 13 years ago. It was the longest time I had had to work, uninterrupted, on what Munro would call my "real work." It was also free; I was there as a guest of the Saskatchewan Writer's Guild, which uses the Abbey for a writers' colony — or retreat, as it's often called — during June and July.

And it was absolutely wonderful, every minute of it. I managed to write two short stories. I read more books than I usually read in three months. I got plenty of sleep, took long walks, ate leisurely meals and talked to the other writers. But these concrete activities are really a minor part of what the two weeks meant for me. The majority of my time was spent in that daydreamy, meandering sort of activity that Munro describes so perfectly as the "wooing of distant parts of myself." It's the feeling of having your brain "unkink," sort of, just as your body does in a hot bath after strenuous exercise, so that you can explore all those half-thoughts and gleams and wishes that seem too flighty and too irrelevant for everyday life, but which are often the germ of a good poem or the beginning of a short story.

St. Peter's gave me time. It also gave me silence. The section where the writers are quartered observes absolute silence every day from 9 a.m. to 4:30 p.m., with the exception of a half-hour lunch break. There was no one to talk to, no telephones to answer, no radios, no TV. This in itself was a gift, but the Abbey is also situated on 2,500 acres of farmland. A walk in any direction took me through fields of vegetables and flowers, always surrounded by the tall pines that serve as wind-breaks. Or, I could walk through the woodland areas where one of the monks maintains paths that twist and turn through groves of poplar and willow, open into meadows or a "bee-loud glade" where the hives are kept, until I reached the wheat fields and the open prairie sky.

There is no question that at least *some* time to live like this is essential to any creative work. It is equally obvious that, until this century at least, the opportunity for such a life was closed to all but a very few. And of those few, only a handful were women. And of those few women, virtually none was like myself, with children and jobs *in addition to* their writing. Flannery O'Connor, Joyce Carol Oates, Katherine Mansfield, Dorothy Parker, to name only four of the many distinguished women writers of this century, have all been childless. Those who did have children — Margaret Laurence, Alice Munro — speak of the difficulties of trying to do both, while others, like Sylvia Plath, committed suicide partly out of the despair that grew from not being able to.

Yet, although *some* contemplative life is a necessity for a writer, it can also be a limitation. After two weeks at St. Peter's I began to understand this more completely than I ever had. After two weeks of not hearing a child's voice, for example, I could see why those children in Victoria novels always sound so *unchildlike*. They exist on the page as they existed for the author — beings one saw briefly, when their nanny brought them down after dinner, perhaps, but never as people one had to *live* with. After two weeks of eating food I didn't shop for or prepare, I began to understand why so many dinners in so many novels seem to appear out of thin air. And no wonder Doris Lessing's *The Golden Notebook* was so popular when it first appeared in 1962. It contained a famous passage in which an ordinary woman's day was described in detail, a woman who actually had to work for a living, shop, prepare food, and care for her child, in addition to trying to write.

So, yes, St. Peter's was wonderful, and re-entry into ordinary life is difficult; the phone and the TV are much too loud; everyone drives too fast. And, yes, I'll go back again. But, no, I wouldn't want that sort of life all the time. I know that in much of the literature from the past, however beautiful it is, there is something essential missing and that that lack arises directly from a lack in the life of the writer, a lack as serious as that of not having enough time. One of the challenges for me as a writer is to put some of what is missing, some of the messy details by which most of us live our lives, finally, on the page.

■ ■ ■ ■ ■

Reader Response Makes the 'Isolated' Writer Feel Integral to Community

"What do you call a woman driver?" the voice behind me asks.
Women driver? Wha — ?

I'm standing in the produce section of Loblaws, trying to decide which grapefruit is the best deal. The woman who's laughing as I turn around is someone I know only as a face at parent meetings at my son's school or a quick "hello" if we pass on the street. Why is she asking me riddles all of a sudden? "Someone who drives like a man and gets blamed for it," she chortles. "Maybe you can use that sometime, eh?" And before I can say anything more than a confused "ah — gee — thanks," she's already turning her cart toward the lettuce.

"I really like your column," she smiles over her shoulder, "keep up the good work."

And later that week, as I'm leaving the bank, someone else comes to me. "I liked your piece last week," she says, "but I don't agree with you when you say . . . . "

She takes a few minutes to offer me an argument I hadn't considered before. Enough material, almost, for a whole other column on the topic, which I hope to get around to after I do the piece on Women and Food that Pat suggested, which will be sometime after I've worked up that material that Jim sent in the mail last month, which I'm sure I can get to as soon as . . . .

When all I wrote was poetry, I used to think of writing as an extremely solitary occupation. And not just because I had to be alone in the room to do it well, either. Making a good poem takes hours of uncluttered, uninterrupted time in which to perfect a kind of deepening concentration, a gradual "shutting out" of this world so that I can more fully experience the world I'm making on the page, the world you'll have to believe in if a poem is going to be accessible to you. Of course, my family will tell you that all I ever do is sit in my study drinking coffee, staring moodily out of the window, mumbling to myself, but that's because they're jealous of how perfectly I've learned to ignore them.

When the poem's finally done I can emerge into the country of "what's for dinner" and live quite peaceably — until it's time to write another. By that time, the earlier poem's forgotten, stuck into a sheaf of paper somewhere. Two or three years pass before they all show up in a book.

"What? Did I write these?" I think when I see them, turning each one over in my mind as I would a snapshot from a vacation I took years ago. "Was I, really ever *there*? Really? It can't be."

The rhythm of writing poetry, as you can see, is a very leisurely one. And that adds again to the sense of solitude. It's only when a book comes out — and then for only a few weeks — that I get any sense of anyone out there actually reading the stuff. I get to give a few readings; I read some reviews. I have a sense of a conversation, begun years ago, finally completing itself as words or questions that I put forward earlier finally receive a response.

Writing this column, though, is a very different matter. It still requires concentration, quiet and solitude ("and," I can hear my family saying, "the coffee and the mumbling and the staring out the window") but then, a week or so later, there it is, in print. And there are the people, people who live in the same city I live in, taking the time to tell me what they think of it. My sense of being involved in an extended communal conversation grows weekly as readers respond to what I say and I incorporate their ideas into my next piece and they have something to say about that . . . .

This particular fall, my sense of involvement is even stronger. I continue to have the regular, almost neighborly, response to my column and I am beginning to hear some reaction to a new book of poems, just out a few weeks ago. I've been traveling a lot in the last 10 days, giving readings and interviews, conducting high-school workshops about my book. It's great to hear a group of grade nines talk about how one poem (about my son) could easily be about them or to have someone come up to me after a reading and say, "Your poems made me feel as if you've been following me around for the last few years."

All of this praise does wonders for my ego, of course, but there's something else happening as well. I'm beginning to see just how much readers' responses, even the negative ones, make me feel part of the local community in which I live and the wider community in which I write. They make my work with words, those difficult, airy things, seem as concrete as the work that goes into producing the food and clothing and furniture we also need to get along. It's a good feeling — and a necessary one — since it helps to break down the isolation I often feel.

Writing this column has also helped me to appreciate how much my readers' response contributes to my work, how much I use what people tell me about a poem or a column in writing the next one. Sometimes this is a matter of looking at a theme or an issue from a new point of view because of what someone else has said. The conversation we are having expands, grows more complex. It could go on for quite a while.

Which is okay by me. I've got a nice quiet study here. Now, if you'll just wait while I make a fresh pot of coffee . . . .

■ ■ ■ ■ ■

"The Landscape from How I See My Poems Moving": An Interview with Bronwen Wallace

This interview was taped on February 22, 1989 just before Bronwen Wallace read at Common Woman Books in Edmonton. Our discussion was fiercely pleasurable and I was moved and instructed by Bronwen's toughminded commitment to her community and to the grain of the local. The feminist politics and poetics which emerge in this conversation are grounded in the gritty pain of many women's everyday lives and insist on the differential specificity of women's experience.

While Bronwen stayed with me, she rested in the afternoon, apologizing that her health was temporarily complicated. Like so many others, I filled up with grief on learning of her cancer and later, her painful death. Bronwen made several editorial excisions in the original interview manuscript and these passages have been omitted. After Bronwen's death her literary executor, Carolyn Smart, completed the editing in consultation with Chris Whynot. I am grateful to them for their attentiveness to the text which conveys some of the passion for women's words and empowerment informing Bronwen's voice.

Janice Williamson

JANICE WILLIAMSON: Your work focuses on women's lives. How have you developed an understanding of the community of women and the daily language which women speak?

BRONWEN WALLACE: Some of this just comes from my own experience. My parents came from the farm, so I grew up around rural people and working-class people who tell stories. Some of that language comes from what I remember of all those conversations and people telling stories. The other big influence is that I've been a feminist since 1969. Some of what happens in my poems is an attempt to capture how women's conversations work, which is never linear but circles and moves around things. It's really important for me to try and capture conversational English, to make the poem as accessible as possible, to make it seem as though what's happening is really mundane. I started out thinking that story was everything that mattered, that what happened was all the poem was about, and now I see that the story is an extended metaphor for the voice of discovery and the mystery within what happens. That's how the poems have changed in terms of that narrative.

JW: You've lived and worked in the area around Kingston in southern Ontario all of your life. How much of that region is in your work?

BW: A lot, a lot. I personally could not separate the landscape from the way people talk, and I couldn't separate the landscape from how I see my poems moving. In my head my poems try to replicate the landscape of southern Ontario which appears mundane, straight and ordinary, though I think it's quite surreal and magical.

JW: Are there other writers in the area whom you identify as having a particular regional aesthetic?

BW: The person who had the most direct influence on me was Al Purdy. I went all the way through half of a Ph.D. in English and never,

ever read Canadian writing, never, ever read a Canadian poem. I spent all of those years at Queen's hearing people put it down as unimportant. So when I first started to write, I wrote bad T.S. Eliot. Then in 1970 I quit school and hitchhiked around Canada. I was in a Vancouver bookstore and found a copy of *The Cariboo Horses*. I remember reading "The Country North of Belleville" and it was like one of those kind of intense — like it was a religious experience! I remember I was actually crying, because it never occurred to me that it was possible and okay to write about those people in that kind of language. My poems move in a different way than Al Purdy's. His move very conversationally; the associations or leaps that I make are different. Another important person for me was Alice Munro, obviously, in terms of respecting the landscape and the way people talked.

JW: This is a similar question, but from a different location. You've been thinking as a feminist since 1969 and writing seriously since about 1975. You've participated in the women's movement during an incredible cultural explosion of women's writing, of women thinking and writing about women writing. How do you locate yourself as a writer in this new feminist landscape inhabited by women's bookstores filled with provocative ideas and a sophisticated critical vocabulary?

BW: Personally, as someone who's also an activist, it's really exciting to see this happening; it's really exciting to be part of that history in the present. There is also an increasing feeling of support and safety to try different things, a certain real sense of community. In the last ten years, I've become excited by the range of voices from Daphne Marlatt or Di Brandt to someone like me whom you might regard as a much more conservative writer in terms of the kinds of experiments I'm willing to do with language. I see this as a big choir; everybody has her part; I'm really excited by all the different and valuable ways women are writing. I know that I couldn't do what Daphne does but obviously she can't do what I do. I'm also interested in the development of feminist theory, because writing is very, very lonely. You put out this stuff but with theory it comes back to you connected to the world in a different way.

JW: Your notation of a choir, of a politics of difference and diversity, has been enriched by black women speaking out and saying, "You white women, whether you're working-class or middle-class, have not enabled us to speak, and you have not heard us." How particular is your voice coming from a rural working-class, white . . .

BW: What I've got to say comes out of those roots, but it's from someone who's also had a lot more education than my parents had. I had really strong feelings about the Women's Press debate. As I understand the debate, women of color are saying, we don't want you to write in our voice because we don't get a chance to write in our own voice because this is a racist country and we don't get published. This is a real world issue, not something in our heads about our imagination. It's about who gets published and who doesn't. I don't see it as censorship; we're being asked to stand in solidarity with women of color. It particularly bothers me when white women equivocate on that issue because we're always talking about the same issue. Henry James did such a great job in representing a woman's experience in *Portrait of a Lady*. *Portrait of a Lady* is certainly one of my favorite novels, but why didn't Henry James bring all that sensitivity to bear on the character of Gilbert Osmond and look at what it was like to be all of the things that he knew how to be — male and upper-class in that society? What would have happened if he had? We don't have a portrait of a man that has the kind of accuracy and the wholeness that Jane Austen brought to bear on somebody like Emma. Why do we see limitation as something negative rather than as what we are?

JW: Your concern with violence against women is carried into some of your poems. Elly Danica and Sylvia Fraser have recently written very difficult accounts of their own experiences of child sexual abuse. How do you write about violence against women?

BW: I can only write about my own experience of it so I was very careful in the "Bones" poems to write as a shelter worker. I don't have the right to write as someone who was battered. I don't think we should kid ourselves. As it becomes more socially respectable to be a social worker who works with abused women, the language is starting to change. Now social workers talk about 'conflictive' families or 'spousal abuse' and, once again, feminist language is going to get co-opted. Just telling the stories is essential — one novel is not enough.

JW: Your beautiful title *The Stubborn Particulars of Grace* ranges over just those contradictions between a language of transcendence and a concrete apprehension of the everyday. The everydayness of things provides a poetics and politic in your work.

BW: Essentially it's how I see the world. George MacDonald wrote a children's story called "The Shadow Dancers" in which a man is taken to shadowland. When he comes back, everything looks different. MacDonald says that's how we know that this was a true vision because as he went by the true vision he saw that common things are wonderful, whereas if he'd had a false vision he would have found that common things are commonplace. That is how I really see the world. *The Stubborn Particulars of Grace* is an attempt to begin to talk about spiritual matters in a political context and to say that if we're going to live in a state of grace, if we're going to live with wholeness or integrity in the world, we have to pay attention to the particulars and politics of where we are. You can't be the transcendent God who saves the world by getting out of it. I'm very interested in goddess worship and witchcraft, that sense of the godhead as immanent. I'm also involved right now in the Kingston Coordinating Committee against Domestic Assault on Women (CCADOW) which sets up liaisons between shelters and police and men who are working with abusers and tries to do public education.

JW: How do you link these parts of yourself? Is there a relation between your writing and social change? You write the feminist column for the Kingston *Whig-Standard* and you work with women's groups and write poetry and fiction. Are these separate activities?

BW: No, I see them as connected. Others have asked me this question before so I can quote W.B. Yeats who said, "The arguments I have with others I call rhetoric. The arguments I have with myself I call poetics." When I'm writing my column or doing public education, those are the arguments I have with others, the places where I take a certain position and I'm rhetorical and persuasive. That's one of the things language can do for us. At the other end of the continuum are the internal argu-ments which are in many ways more complex and may not come up with the theoretically correct stance, you usually end up writing really bad poetry, because that's a Stalinism of imagination. But both posi-tions are essential to understanding my place in the world.

JW: Could you elaborate on the limitations of a 'purely theoretical stance?' I assume you mean something that isn't politically engaged in some fundamental way?

BW: Yes. The academic feminists who make me nervous are those who are not engaged in the world, who just sit and write some interesting papers about feminist thought but have never talked to a waitress in their lives. If feminism goes that way, we'll end up like Marxism. At Queen's University a few weeks ago, there was the possibility of a strike and according to my friend in the History Department, Marxist historians were the least clear about what they were going to do because they could do theory but no longer engage with the world — which is a choice. You've got two choices: one of them is to support the oppressed; the other one is to not.

JW: As an academic feminist, I imagine my engagement with the world as, in part, trying to change the academy itself. I want to work with others and make it a place where alternate programs like Women's Studies or alternative pedagogies within traditional disci-plines can stimulate students and others to think critically about fem-inist issues, and to act, and to change. That's the ideal, though it's often not possible to touch more than a handful of students each year.

BW: I see academic feminism as important as long as it recognizes its class privilege, doesn't shut out other women and recognizes what it's doing is not all of feminism.

JW: There is a really strong community of women intellectuals who focus on feminist theory in a very actively engaged way.

BW: That's great. There's also a very strong community of women who focus on pay equity. I'm part of a very strong community of women that is focusing on domestic violence and child abuse. What really burns my ass is when a few academics try to tell me there's only one way to write, or one way to think about the world, or that all my writing and thinking has to be poststructuralist. I react to this in the same way that when I was in the Left I reacted to male Stalinists telling me that there was only one way to read Marx. I say bullshit to that. Sometimes when I hear feminist debates about theory, I hear my days on the Left when a bunch of men sat around and talked about Mao versus Stalin. Who needs it?

JW: But with your interest in voice, and the source of the voice, aren't these different conversations in part because they have different relationships to authority?

BW: Yeah, except in terms of where they stand in relation to dominant society, there is some similarity between a white male radical from the 1960s and a woman with a Ph.D. in a university. There are similarities as well as differences. I only have problems with theoretical debates when they become prescriptive.

JW: In your most recent book, you have a poem, "Joseph MacLeod Daffodils," which is dedicated to another wonderful Ontario writer, Isabel Huggan. It begins, "I'm planting perennials this year, you tell me, because I'm scared it's the only way I know to tell myself I'm going to be here years from now watching them come up." And the poem goes on to address ageing, and the conundrum of the middle-aged woman. I'm edging towards forty and that very strange location where we shift between a pre-written cultural text and the possibilities we imagine for ourselves. Can you talk about that?

BW: For me, the contradiction is that this is the time in my life when I feel the most powerful and the most together and the most on top of things, and it's a time when I'm also most aware of how incredibly misogynous this culture is, even in terms of how this culture treats ageing women. It does happen to men to some extent, but not with anywhere near the same intensity. I have all these images of how women are disempowered and brutalized simply because they're ageing and I'm also much more aware of the kind of power that women have. It's an odd kind of balance. Another aspect for me is in my relationship to young women; I find that their hopefulness is both touching and frustrating. Seven years ago a woman who had been my closest friend for a number of years died of cancer at 33. She was sick for five years before she died and left four very, very small children. We spent all of the available time we could together, and I took care of her during the last three weeks of her life. I learned an awful lot about living from her, but I also learned what I could call a feminist way of dying. One of the things I really notice as I get older is how much more I need the feminist community and how important it is to develop a feminist understanding of death and dying in the face of the denial and technological nightmare that the medical profession is built on — denial of the body. There's so much power in the body. If we would learn to attend to the power, we would learn not to fear what our bodies do. It's connected to how we see the body of the earth; by denying that we're part of the body of the earth, we're going to kill it.

JW: How do you as a female poet represent the female body when it has been constructed in patriarchal language in traditional discourse and connected with the earth in a very objectified way?

BW: The voice in my poems is tremendously important, it's always very clearly a female voice. In using female anecdote as a metaphor for human experience, I see myself in a simple way assuming that a female view of the world could be a human view of the world. Underneath that is the belief that if we don't listen to this voice, we're not going to be here to have any view of the world. The book I'm working on now which I have just barely started is very different than my writing until now, much more public and much less personal. I have a whole series of poems called "Everyday Science" based on 'scientific' facts from the tabloids of *People* magazine. So I'm having a great time, because that's how people understand the world, I mean, that's where we get our facts, right? Another section has to do with our relationships to other animals. I'm a big Vicky Hearne fan. She's a poet and animal trainer, and has a lot of really interesting essays. Her *Adam's Task* is about our relationship to other animals and our sheer arrogance in assuming what other animals understand of the world. The "Koko" poem in *Stubborn Particulars* is a beginning of that. The whole debate, the ludicrous fact that intellectuals, like Noam Chomsky of all people, think that apes can't talk comes out of the sheer patriarchal arrogance that also strip-mines.

JW: These poems seem to provide a populist sociology of knowledge, to help us connect how people think through the popular knowledge they read.

BW: That's right. The first section of poems that I've already finished is a series of poems for — I'm a born-again country music fan. I listened to rock and roll for 25 years, and I just got real tired of men masturbating into their guitars. Somebody gave me "Trio," a great country album with Linda Ronstadt, Dolly Parton, and Emmy Lou Harris, and I fell in love with Emmy Lou Harris. I've been working on a series of poems for Emmy Lou Harris about country music. What interests me is the fact that country music uses a really traditional style; they don't deconstruct anything. But in country music you have people like K.T. Oslin singing love songs like "I'm Always Coming Home to You" to a kid. In her video, she's a mother who does not have custody and can only see her kid on the weekends. In another one called "Child Support," a woman talks about how no matter what happens to her, she always has her child's support. The voices of these women singing about the world from their point of view and assuming that their perspective is going to be accepted fascinates me. That's what I try to do in my poems. I don't think I have the kind of talent to expand it very much with language, but I've consciously chosen not to draw attention to the fact that I'm just matter of factly assuming that a feminist philosophy is part of the world and to be accepted by my reader as common sense. That's what I want to have happen.

JW: The title of your recent book of short stories is *People You'd Trust Your Life To*. How much of that world is informed by feminism, how much do you think your poems appeal to 'traditional' values associated with community and rural familiar values?

BW: You mean, whom am I talking to?

JW: Yes, whom are you talking to, and also I'm curious about the appropriation of feminist language by the right-wing.

BW: Anything can be appropriated by the right-wing; I don't see that as my concern. Lao Tsu says that you have to treat every person as if they were wounded. I'm writing to the wounded part of each person, men as well as women. The power of feminism is the power of the victim who has recognized a way to use her damage. There's a great line in an Adrienne Rich poem about knowing that her wound came from the same place as her power. When you get in touch with your damage, recognize and care for it, you also discover the source of your power. We know that abusers, men who batter, or anybody who abuses children, have usually been abused themselves and have denied it. It's the denial of our damage, our limitations, our vulnerability, our morality that's got us where we are. The voice I try to speak is speaking to that person. I think we're kidding ourselves if we think there's any form of writing that can't be picked up by monopoly capitalism, and that includes any kind of experimental deconstructive writing. Look what's happening in rock and roll on video, all that is being picked up.

JW: The process of writing for you seems to be a laboratory which feeds you with new questions and material for the next project. You talk about your poetry as narrative poetry. What's the transformation in working on your short stories?

BW: I always thought there was a major difference. The poems aren't about what happens but about what's discovered. The narratives in my poems are like guide posts towards a mystery at the center of any story, the mystery of our existence or the mystery of our personality. In the poems, the voice is trying to discover this as it moves through the poem. Starting to write short stories was literally a gift; I was standing in a line-up at Swiss Chalet and a woman started talking to me in my head. I wrote that story and once she told me her story then a number of other women did and I became interested in expanding character. One of the things that makes my poetry strong is a very recognizable voice. In the stories I try to expand that voice. It's a first collection and has its weaknesses but it has taught me some interesting things about voice that I'm now able to apply to the new poems.

[*Pause*]

JW: Okay, we're talking again after your reading at Common Woman Books. At the beginning of your reading tonight you read a Gwendolyn MacEwen poem and talked about how you like to evoke the memory of people who aren't here any longer. Why do you invoke other voices?

BW: I feel strongly that my voice is only one voice in a huge community. It's important to remember that this community includes the dead as well as the living so every time I read I start with a poem by someone who is dead. I started doing it last September as a result of Barrie Nichol's death. I gave a reading at Western just after he died and I began that reading with a poem of his. Gwen died, and Raymond Carver died in the summer — people who had been really important to me.

JW: You seem to generate some of your poems through other voices in epigraphs or quotation. Could you talk about that procedure?

BW: That's something I started doing in *The Stubborn Particulars of Grace* and obviously I'm moving on with that in the Emmy Lou Harris poems with quotations from country songs. But a lot of the references are not a direct quote but are echoed so that if you know country music you're going to know the quote. It's a way of deepening the poem for me and a way of evoking other voices. We do this in conversation. We say, I was reading so-and-so, or so-and-so said . . . . I'm trying to bring as many voices into the conversation as I possibly can. In *Stubborn Particulars* it's quite literary. Somebody who doesn't listen to country music read a rough draft of the Emmy Lou Harris poems and said that they couldn't hear the music. Sharon Thesen has a wonderful series of poems based on Matisse paintings; it's assumed when you read those poems that you know the Matisse paintings. This is in no way criticism, but reading is based on certain assumptions which are located in a particular class, in a particular relationship to a particular kind of art. In my case, not everybody is going to know country music but there are reasons for that and I think we have to look at the reasons.

JW: At the reading tonight, a woman prefaced her question with a self-deprecating "This might be an ignorant question, but . . . ." Then she asked a wonderful question that came from her immediate response to the poems. How do you respond to that?

BW: That makes my day. That's what I do it for and it's much more important to me than, say, a good review, because I get the sense that in some way she's taken those poems into her life. That's what I want to have happen and that really matters. It's especially great when somebody says, "Oh, I don't like poetry" or "I don't know anything about poetry but . . . ." I try to make my poetry popular and accessible so when somebody finds it that way, I know I'm on the right track.

JW: You wrote what you call a love poem, but a male reviewer called it a "feminist rant."

BW: Anger is one of the stories we have to tell. We have lots to be angry about, and feeling safe or strong or sure enough to be able to reveal our intense anger is part of what the feminist community has done for women in our 'take back the night' marches or our speak-outs. We can admit, like Robin Morgan says, to an almost intolerable rage of being female in North America in the 20th century and know that we're not going to be ostracized for it, that we're in a community that recognizes that there's a reason for our anger. My poems don't always sound as angry as they feel because I assume that the anger is shared.

JW: How confessional are your books? How autobiographical are they?

BW: The separation is becoming greater and greater. The first two books are intensely autobiographical as well as confessional. But in *Stubborn Particulars*, a lot is not autobiographical but stuff I've made up or stolen from other people's lives. I'm creating a persona in *Stubborn Particulars*, a persona who is the best or bravest part of me. She does the talking and has more courage to explore things than I do in my everyday self. In the new book I'm exploring and I'm going to fragment and split up the voices. It's still confessional as voice in that someone will be talking intimately from the details of her life. Confessional poetry does not simply bear the actual autobiographical details of our lives but it can be a particular stance vis-à-vis the reader, a tone of private conversation. When we tell the stories of our lives, we're confessing to each other. That may have religious or spiritual connotations. I was raised as a Protestant so I don't understand the Catholic confessional as institution, but when we tell people intimate things about ourselves we are in some way asking for, if not absolution, at least support, inclusion, something, a healing gesture from the other person. That's why we confess. And so I see that it's part of what I was saying about wounds and damage — it's another way of opening yourself up to the other person. This goes far beyond the confessional as we've understood it in autobiography. When Lowell wrote 'confessional poetry' he wasn't using it in this sense. For me, it's a request placed on the reader to stand in a certain relation to the speaker.

JW: Your humor works to position the reader within complicitous laughter. Is this a gesture which requires a similar kind of understanding?

BW: I like to make people laugh. Humor is obviously less intimidating and I suppose it is another way of trying to set up some sort of openness between the reader and the speaker. When I'm writing a poem, my image of the reader is not like you and me sitting here talking. When I think of the reader, she or he is not on this side of the poem while I'm on the other side. The reader stands beside me and we're reading the poem together.

JW: What about difference? Your side-by-side reading suggests a process of recognition. What about the spaces where there is no recognition?

BW: The image of two people looking in the same direction does not necessarily mean that they're seeing the same thing. We can be in solidarity and not have the same experience of the world. I can be in solidarity with Salman Rushdie and know that we could be totally opposed on a whole bunch of other issues. In his essay "The Storyteller," John Berger talks about storytelling in the peasant community where he lives now. Although the stories in this community do carry judgment, they're always told with the awareness that the person who's telling the story will live in the community with the person he's telling the story about all of his or her life. This affects all the individual responses to the story and not in a negative way; it's not censorship but a certain kind of tolerance, kindliness, a desire to withhold judgment which does not necessarily mean that you don't still marvel at the mystery of the story. This is connected to what I was saying about the confession; we can tell each other about our lives recognizing that we're going to be inextricably connected as long as we're human beings on this earth. And in the best possible world, this affects how the story's heard too.

Coda:
Blueprints For A Larger Life

I decided to call my talk "Blueprints for a Larger Life" because it seems to me that the idea of a blueprint involves both the ability to express imaginatively, in the language of architecture, what we want to create, and at the same time recognizes that the blueprint must pay attention to such physical realities as gravity, weather, and the nature of concrete or wood. Otherwise, the building, like the poem, collapses.

So this is going to be a very physical talk. What I want to do is evoke the bodies of women, as I would in a poem. I want to use our bodies as a guide to understanding why we are here today. I want it to be through our bodies, our presence as women, that we understand both aspects of International Women's Day, protest and celebration.

Let's begin with my body, and what it means to have me standing up here, talking to you out there. For one thing, I'm here, in this room with you, sharing these ideas. Given the centuries of women's silence, my presence here is something to celebrate. So is yours.

However, my presence here is a particular, specific, physical one. I am middle-aged, middle-class, white, heterosexual. The specific details of my physical presence are both a limitation and a strength in terms of what I will say, and in what I cannot. It is important for us to think about how my speech would change if I were a woman of color, if I spoke to you from a wheelchair, or if — wonder of wonders — I signed my speech and the other person on the stage said it out loud for the "signing impaired."

Each of us then, by our physical presence, represents both possibility and limitation. And when I talk about our presence as women, I want us to understand it in the widest possible terms, so that our presence here today evokes the presence of other women, both living and dead, who have made such a day possible. That includes the garment workers who organized the original March 8th demonstration for equal rights and safer working conditions; women who have worked for education, reproductive choice, suffrage, and pay equity; the women who made the clothes we are wearing, and the furniture we are using; the women who help to keep this building clean, warm, and well-lighted.

Let's bring some other voices in at this point, some more physical presences. First, I want to evoke presences from our most ancient past, to read from one of the oldest oral traditions, and one of the oldest religions still in existence. I want to read from the Liturgy of the Craft (Wicca, Witchcraft), from part of the section called The Charge of the Goddess. I cannot think of anything more celebratory and powerful than these words:

> Let My worship be in the heart that rejoices, for behold — all acts of love and pleasure are My rituals. Let there be beauty and strength, power and compassion, honor and humility, mirth and reverence within you. And you who seek to know Me, know that your seeking and yearning will avail you not, unless you know the Mystery: for if that which you seek, you find not within yourself, you will never find it without. For behold, I have been with you from the beginning, and I am that which is attained at the end of desire.

The power suggested there is some small indication of the power we have lost, as women, but it is also a testimony to the power that is ours. It is important to recognize that the understanding of power inherent in the Liturgy is a conception of power as *immanent*, power from within, *power to*. The power that we face most often in our culture, however, is *power over*: the power of men over women, adults over children, whites over blacks, rich over poor, humans over nature.

I want to evoke more bodies at this point. I am thinking of the bodies of women who are beaten by their partners, of women who are raped, the bodies of prostitutes, and the passive body of the centerfold and the porno film. I think of how body language (stronger even than the conscious mind) is often the only clue to incest and child abuse. I think of the bodies of women who work all day and still cannot support their children, and of others who work all day and for that reason lose custody of their children — because they are not "fit mothers."

I remember the bodies of anorexics who in starving themselves act out the unreality, the lack of satisfaction that lies at the heart of our society of consumption (this idea comes from an article by Maggie Helwig, a poet and a recovered anorexic, published in *This Magazine*). I think of the bodies of homeless "bag ladies," and the millions of bodies of the "two-thirds world" women and their children, who even as I say these words, are dying of hunger. There are women in every country whose bodies are worn out, twisted, maimed, and diseased because of the work they must do. And I want also to evoke the bodies of women long dead, whose lives left no trace, and whose history is the history of a silence so vast that it seems impossible that there will ever be enough anecdotes and letters and songs and shouts and cries and stories and poems to fill it.

"A Poem About Rape" by Libby Scheier is about that silence, about the difficulty, the great work of making our presence known. As is often the case in women's writing, it does so by evoking the presence of one specific woman, in one specific situation. In doing it well, it speaks for all of us. Here are the last three stanzas:

How can I explain rape to someone
who finds a one-a.m. streetcar ride alone
boring, how can I explain that

some people find it frightening?
How can I explain rape to someone
who does not worry about who gets on
the streetcar, who looks at you,
who gets off when you do.

It's hard to write a poem about rape.
I don't want to write a political tract.
I want you to grasp the experience.
I don't think a poem can do that.
Certainly this poem is not doing it.
This poem is definitely a failure
in bringing the experience of rape
into your living room.

A dramatic re-enactment is not the answer.
A film about rape is not the answer.
These usually excite you anyway
which is not my purpose.
Raping you is not the answer.
There doesn't seem to be any answer.
There doesn't seem to be any answer right now.

What I like about this poem is the way it uses the limitation imposed on it — the impossibility of writing a poem about rape — to, in fact, write a poem about rape. And to write a poem that is more than "simply" a description of the crime, a poem that speaks to the way in which women's suffering is silenced in this culture, trivialized by the courts and by movies and novels in which rape is seen as "not all that serious." What I like is the way the poet uses her damage as protest, shoves her life into the face of the patriarchy and says, "You better listen to this." I like the way it ends on the line, "There doesn't seem to be any answer right now." I put a lot of emphasis on the "right now."

This is the form of protest we engage in, together, in such events as "speak outs" and Take Back The Night marches. Part of the power of those events grows from the power of our presence as real, specific women. It's power we can feel, power that comes from within, from using the damage and suffering we have experienced to make ourselves present to those who have tried to silence us. And it is interesting, particularly in light of some of the reactions to this year's Take Back The Night march, how threatening the presence of women's bodies, of women's suffering, can be. If we're not present in the "ladylike" way — if our presence is not an "absence of power," in other words — then, even for one night, for one march, our power is a threat. In fact one measure of the power of our presence in this culture is the violence of the reaction to it.

Perhaps this is most clearly evident today in the area of reproductive choice. And in many ways it is this area of our lives as women, more than any other, in which the possibility of our realizing our full power is most threatening to a patriarchal culture. And it is in this area that the push to erase women — our bodies, the specificity of our lives — is going to be most strong.

And that is exactly what is happening. Look at what has happened to the debate on abortion since the Supreme Court decision last year. It has almost exclusively narrowed itself down to an issue of the "rights" of the fetus versus the "rights" of the woman. A situation of incredible human complexity has been framed as a mathematical problem. An issue that involves, in each individual instance such diverse considerations as class, race, relative economic power, age, available health care, access to birth control, access to jobs, day care, good doctors, education and physical, mental and spiritual well-being is being expressed in our culture as an issue of "rights," as if all "rights" were the same and everybody was equal.

Now let's think about what this means for a moment. Let's think about who's setting the agenda here. Let's think about what's missing — or rather who's missing: women's bodies again, women's lives.

That is what happens when the issue is framed as an equation — fetal rights=women's rights. Women's bodies get left out. The hard,

stubborn fact that a fetus is part of a woman's body — and cannot survive without a woman's body — gets left out. The hard, stubborn fact
that life depends on women's bodies gets left out; or rather, it becomes
an issue for control, for power over, which is the only kind of power
this culture understands.

What the abortion debate comes down to, as our culture sees it, is
who is going to have power over human life. And because our culture
sees it that way, the abortion issue can only be "resolved" by ensuring
that the state has power over women's bodies. Public sentiment — 69
per cent of the population support abortion at least in the early stages of
pregnancy — may force it to curtail that power; but that is still the issue.

This becomes increasingly evident, of course, when we look at
other aspects of reproductive control currently being exercised in our
society: surrogate motherhood; fertility experiments; *in utero* opera-
tions; legal actions that force women to undergo certain medical pro-
cedures (e.g. Caesarean section) against their will, to protect the life
of the fetus; increased technological control of natural births; enforced
(or strongly encouraged) sterilization of poor women and women of
color; the use of dangerous drugs to "control populations" in the two-
thirds world as a way of solving what is called the "population problem;" the fact that lesbian couples have little or no access to
fertilization programs available to heterosexual couples.

In all of these cases the issue is power, and since our culture
understands power as *power over*, it's not surprising that women who
want abortions get portrayed as frivolous sluts who would kill a baby
so that they don't have to miss a Take Back The Night march. If
you're deluded into thinking that you can have power over everything in this world, including human life, you're likely to believe that.

But what happens if we put women's bodies into the picture?
Women's bodies, and women's lives, in all their maddeningly specific,
frustratingly complex detail? What happens then? If you want to
know, read the poem "Christmas Carols" by Margaret Atwood to discover what a difference the presence of women's bodies makes.

What's happened to our neat equation now? Now, rather than

talking about whether women have the right to destroy life, we're talking about why we are in situations of unwanted pregnancy at all. Which, of course, is a much deeper question, a question that asks us to recognize the *power to*, the power that comes from within, the power that must work with the political and material limitations and possibilities of real bodies, in real cultures.

Women have always had to deal with this question, of course. Rather than having power *over* life and death, we have recognized that we have only the power to ensure that life continues. The full realization of that power is, and has always been, a tremendous responsibility. As Germaine Greer points out in *Sex and Destiny*, motherhood "is a bloody business from the first menstruations through pregnancies, births, miscarriages, infant deaths and the frequent deaths of mothers themselves. Besides the virtues of tenderness, patience, and self-forgetfulness, a mother had to exercise courage, determination and decisiveness." She goes on to point out that, historically, it has been women who have had to maintain the right balance between the number of children and the food supply, women who have practiced infanticide in situations where starvation was inevitable.

Today, at least in this culture (and indeed, only in this culture), starvation may not be the primary motive for abortion. But for most women it is still an attempt to realize the power that Greer alludes to. This is not the power over life and death, as patriarchal culture understands power, but the power to ensure the best life for her unborn child, for other children she may have, for other people in her life, for herself. That's why we have to ask the question, why are there unwanted children at all?

Where is our power to avoid unwanted pregnancies when we still do not have equal access to safe, effective birth control? When even the most obvious form of birth control, abstinence, is seldom — given the sexual power games in this culture — at the command of every woman?

Where is our power to ensure the sanctity of life when vast numbers of children are routinely raped and abused and when millions of children on this planet are starving to death?

Where is our power to ensure safety for our children when the same government that would deny us the option of abortion actively supports a military philosophy which could destroy every living thing on this planet?

And we cannot talk about abortion and reproductive choice in this culture without evoking the bodies of children, as well as the bodies of women. They are inseparable. And in this culture, children are even more absent than women. Everywhere the message that they are not welcome is clear. Breast-feeding is not accommodated easily in most public places. Children's noise is frowned upon. There are many apartment buildings where they are not welcome. This is a society that talks at length about protecting the fetus and then does everything in its power to oppress and destroy the child.

I have talked at length about abortion because I believe it is linked, inextricably, to fundamental issues of life and power. You might say that the debate around abortion is a microcosm of the dilemma we find ourselves in as a species. It is a debate about the nature of our power. It is a life and death debate.

In demanding that women's bodies and women's lives, children's bodies and children's needs be deeply present in the debate around abortion, we are demanding that our culture face up to what its misuse of power, as power over mothers, has made of this society. It has created a society where women do not want to have children, a society that does not welcome children.

What is happening in our culture is part of the misuse of power globally, seen also in the control by consumer nations of the "two-thirds world," and in human arrogance about our place as one species among many on a very small planet. White industrialized patriarchal power has created a situation where all life may soon end. In such a situation, vilifying women for wanting to decide whether or not to bring children into the world is hypocritical in the extreme.

Maybe we need to look at the *real* pro-life option now, at the power that comes from within. We need to look at the *power to*, the power that recognizes a connection between its possibilities and its limitations. By limitations I don't mean something prohibitive or negative, although our usual cultural understanding of power might lead us to conclude that. I mean getting a realistic grip on what we are. I mean all the physical, political, emotional, and spiritual factors involved in deciding what we are capable of as individuals and in our connections to other human beings. That is what a woman has to consider, in considering whether or not to have a child. It's something we need to do as a species, to look at our limitations and our power, our connections to each other, to other animals and to the earth itself.

Abortion is not the only area, of course, where patriarchal culture is currently attempting to find mathematical solutions to human problems. Another example might be child custody and the recent attempts to have enforced joint custody, or enforced mediation in divorce cases. I must say I find it interesting that a culture that devotes so much energy to sentimentalizing "the family" is also a culture that goes for the most legalistic solution to family problems every time, thereby showing its true interests: the maintenance of the patriarchal family. This is the family as business enterprise, the family as institution, with children as assets and commodities.

With this concept of the family, there is nothing wrong with awarding custody to abusive fathers, or, as was recently the case, denying custody to a mother on the grounds that she is "unfit" because she went to a shelter. This is the same logic that sent that child to his father, even though an earlier court had not even allowed this man overnight access. I think that what we are seeing in the area of custody is connected to what we are seeing in the area of reproductive rights. It has little to do with caring for children or wanting safe, positive environments for them to grow up in. It has to do with property, power, and control. It has little to do with loving the kids. The culture that comes up with something like enforced joint custody is the same one that sees nothing wrong with the fact that something like 35,000 children (or however many would fill the CNE stadium) go to bed hungry every night in Toronto alone. It's the same culture that has for centuries sent children off to fight its wars.

It's also a culture that is willing to import babies from areas such as Honduras for the purpose of using their organs for transplants. You may have already heard of the traffic in adult organs, by which peasants in the "two-thirds world" are encouraged to "sell" a kidney for a fee. There are now reports from Brazilian and Honduran papers alleging that mothers in those countries are told that their children have died, when in fact the babies have been sold to families in Canada, Western Europe, and the United States, who supposedly sell their organs for transplants.

That our culture has reached the point where we would participate in the sale of human organs has important ramifications for women. It seems to me that some of the genetic and reproductive research being carried on today can be seen in the same light. It is another aspect of the attempt to exert control over the human body, and particularly to exert control over the bodies of those who are less powerful. It is connected, too, to continued attempts to exert control over the bodies of other animals and over the body of the earth.

When we look at what we're up against in global terms, it sometimes seems impossible that anything can change. And yet one of the reasons we are all here today is that we know, as individual women, in our own particular lives, that change is possible — individual change and collective change. It seems to me that feminism, as a political force in this culture, is one of the main agents for social change at this time, specifically because it connects the individual and the collective, the private and the political. And, for me, it's important to emphasize both. Individual change is, for me, only one aspect of the process because change for individuals always takes place in a social context. It takes place because of a social context.

For me that means a commitment to change that recognizes how the politics of class and race affect feminism. How does it shape the questions we ask, the demands we make? If we look at abortion, for example, we can see that by seeing it simply as a matter of "reproductive choice" we are phrasing the question in white, middle-class terms. There are many women for whom choice is impossible, even under very liberal legislation, because of their poverty and because of their color. Often, the agenda of feminism in this country is still a very middle-class one. As someone once pointed out, the terms "Ms." and "Chairperson" are now almost universally used, but working women still make about 70 per cent of what men earn for the same job.

Another thing to talk about in this context is who our allies are. I remember a poster from the 1960s that showed a black woman leaning against a fence in an inner-city neighborhood. "Class consciousness is knowing which side of the fence you're on," it said. "Class analysis is knowing who's there with you." If you don't like the idea of sides, you might think of Emma Goldman's comment about dancing at your own revolution, and imagine a slogan something like "Class consciousness is knowing who's calling the tune. Class analysis is knowing who's going to dance with you."

I think we all know who's calling the tune. We're not always clear who wants to dance with us. If we were to evoke more bodies at this point, we would certainly, I think, evoke those of our children, our daughters and our sons.

The question of allies raises many questions. Are all women natural allies? Or do we have allies among men as well, particularly men who are working to realize a sense of power within themselves? I myself think that we do. I was particularly taken, for example, with a recent CBC Ideas program about the poet Robert Bly and the men's gatherings that he holds yearly at his farm in the Midwest. I have long been an admirer of Bly's poetry and his interest in goddess figures. It is the interest, in fact, that led him to explore earlier expressions of male power — what he calls "wild men" — power that comes from within, and is not used to control others.

In earlier societies it was common for men and women to get together separately to discover their own powers, their own connections to the god/goddess, to appreciate the strengths and beauties of their own sex, to become friends. Some of that is happening today in women's celebrations like this one, and some situations where men get together in a positive way, to examine how the patriarchy has damaged them. And

it seems to me that that might be a guide for us in determining where
our political alliances lie, and what sort of people are working politically in ways that strengthen us. I see allies among trade union workers,
environmentalists, native rights, and anti-nuke activities, among all
those who want to change the nature of power in this culture.

I want to end with two poems that celebrate the power and presence of women's bodies. Together they say anything that I might have
said in the way of concluding remarks, and they say it much more
powerfully. The first is a poem by Jeni Couzyn, about the importance
of the journey we each make alone, inward, the journey described in
the *Charge to the Goddess*, the journey that discovers a kind of individual power that is not destructive. It also manages to be a very funny
poem and I'm sure you'll recognize the women in it. It's called "House
of Changes":

My body is a wide house
a commune
of bickering women, hearing
their own breathing
denying each other.

Nearest the door
ready in her black leather
is *Vulnerable*. She lives in the hall
her face painted with care
her black boots reaching her crotch
her black hair shining
her skin milky and soft as butter.
If you should ring the doorbell
she would answer
and a wound would open across her eyes
as she touched your hand.

On the stairs, glossy and determined

is *Mindful.* She's the boss, handing out
punishments and rations and examination
papers with precise
justice. She keeps her perceptions in a huge
album under her arm
her debts in the garden with the weedkill
friends in a card-index
on the windowsill of the sitting room
and a tape-recording of the world
on earphones
which she plays to herself over and over
assessing her life
writing summaries.

In the kitchen is *Commendable.*
The only lady in the house who
dresses in florals
she is always busy, always doing something
for someone she has
a lot of friends. Her hands are quick and
cunning as blackbirds
her pantry is stuffed with loaves and fishes
she knows the times of trains and
mends fuses and makes
a lot of noise with the vacuum cleaner.
In her linen cupboard, new-ironed and neatly
folded, she keeps her resentments like
wedding presents — each week
takes them out for counting not to
lose any but would never think of
using any being a lady.

Upstairs in a white room is
my favorite. She is *Equivocal*

has no flesh on her bones
that are changeable as yarrow stalks.
She hears her green plants talking
watches the bad dreams under the world
unfolding
spends all her days and nights
arranging her symbols
never sleeps
never eats hamburgers
never lets anyone into her room
never asks for anything.

In the basement is *Harmful.*
She is the keeper of weapons
the watchdog. Keeps intruders at bay
but the others keep her
locked up in the daytime and when she escapes
she comes out screaming
smoke streaming from her nostrils
flames on her tongue
razor-blades for fingernails
skewers for eyes.

I am *Imminent*
live out in the street
watching them. I lodge myself in other people's
heads with a sleeping bag
strapped to my back.
One day I'll perhaps get to like them enough
these rough, truthful women
to move in. One by one
I'm making friends with them all
unobtrusively, slow and steady
slow and steady.

So that's the individual journey, the one we all make, that often brings us out on a day like today, but we can't make that individual journey, of course, without the political journey as well, the journey that provides the means, the place, and sometimes the basic physical safety, to undertake the individual journey. This is the journey that we make collectively, each of us adding our own particular strengths and skills.

I want to end with a poem by my friend Lorna Crozier, which puts together everything that I've been trying to say very beautifully. It's called "In Praise of Women":

It's not only the women we know,
our friends and sisters, our mothers
climbing the stairs after work,
weariness heavy on their backs. It is also
the women of Greenham Common, their chain
of endurance and belief stretching the heart.
The women of El Salvador, of Nicaragua,
keening for sons and husbands, the lost
villages, the empty places where nothing grows.
The women of Argentina, searching for grandchildren
through the dark pages of their history. The women
of Chile, carrying the faces of the *desaparecidos*
past the soldiers to the gates of torture,
to the cemetery, NN painted on the graves.
The women who walk with stones in their hands,
with numbers on their wrists, with pieces of their
bodies missing. The women, blinded with hoods,
raped and beaten in secret rooms across America.
Though they have been broken, they hold babies,
load guns, wash the bodies of the dead.
Across borders, across oceans
and the endless reach of the prairie,
our sisters, our mothers, our daughters
join hands. These women
make us holy.

Acknowledgements

Without the assistance and co-operation of Bronwen Wallace's literary executor, Carolyn Smart, and the editors and staff of the Kingston *Whig-Standard*, where many of these essays first appeared, and Melanie Dugan of Quarry Press, this book would not exist. The editor gratefully acknowledges their contribution.

Several essays, speeches, and interviews included in *Arguments with the World* have been first printed here or reprinted by permission:

"The Morningside Interviews" were first published in *Open Letter*, Seventh Series No. 9. Winter 1991, and are reprinted by permission of Peter Gzowski.

"The Cuban Missile Crisis and Me" is the text of a speech delivered to the Department of History at the Twenty-first Annual Conference for History and Social Science Teachers at Queen's University, Kingston, Ontario, 6 November 1987, first published here.

"Domestic Violence: What Is the Connection between Home

and School?" is the text of undated address first published here.

"Lilacs in May: A Tribute to Al Purdy" is the text of an undated address first published here.

"Why I Don't (Always) Write Short Stories" was first published in *Quarry Magazine*, Volume 37, Number 3, 1988, and subsequently under the title "A Writer with a Poem to Tell" in *The Whig-Standard Magazine* and in *Quiet Voices: Diverse Essays and Stories from* The Whig-Standard Magazine (Quarry Press / The Whig-Standard).

" 'The Landscape from How I See My Poems Moving': An Interview with Bronwen Wallace" by Janice Williamson first appeared in *Open Letter*, Seventh Series, No. 9, Winter 1991, and is reprinted here by permission of the interviewer.

"Blueprints for a Larger Life" is the text of a keynote address given by Bronwen Wallace at St. Lawrence College in Kingston, Ontario to mark the beginning of International Women's Week in March 1989 first published in *The Whig-Standard Magazine* and in *Quiet Voices: Diverse Essays and Stories from* The Whig-Standard Magazine (Quarry Press /The Whig-Standard).

"Testimonies" and "Koko" from *Stubborn Particulars of Grace* by Bronwen Wallace are reprinted by permission of the Canadian Publishers, McClelland & Stewart, Toronto.

"Into the Midst of It" and "A Simple Poem for Virginia Woolf" from *Common Magic* by Bronwen Wallace are reprinted by permission of Oberon Press.

All other essays included in *Arguments with the World* first appeared in the column "In Other Words" on the editorial pages of *The Whig-Standard*.

Bibliography

Wallace, Bronwen, and Mary di Michele. *Bread and Chocolate / Marrying into the Family*. Ottawa: Oberon Press, 1980.

Wallace, Bronwen. *Signs of the Former Tenant*. Ottawa: Oberon Press, 1983.

_____ *Common Magic*. Ottawa: Oberon Press, 1985.

_____ *The Stubborn Particulars of Grace*. Toronto: McClelland & Stewart, 1987.

_____ *People You'd Trust Your Life To*. Toronto: McClelland & Stewart, 1990.

_____ *Keep That Candle Burning Bright and Other Poems*. Toronto: Coach House Press, 1991.